UNDER GOD'S SKY

*R*eflections for *C*hristian *M*en

John R. Hardison

Northwestern Publishing House
Milwaukee, Wisconsin

Cover photo: ShutterStock, Inc.
Art Director: Karen Knutson
Designer: Pamela Wood

Library of Congress Control Number: 2004104339
Northwestern Publishing House
1250 N. 113th St., Milwaukee, WI 53226-3284
www.nph.net
© 2005 by Northwestern Publishing House
Published 2005
Printed in the United States of America
ISBN-13: 978-0-8100-1674-3
ISBN-10: 0-8100-1674-5

To Benjamin, upon your high school graduation.
Here are some good devotions to read over the summer, and to come back to again and again. Always remember who you are. — Love, your dear sister.

This book is dedicated to the memory of my son,

Gregory Lloyd Hardison,

who helped teach me that

"Jesus is the key to life"

and to my wonderful wife,

Ruth,

who with the Lord's help has stood

by me when I had no right to expect it!

"I know that my Redeemer lives, and that in the end he will stand upon the earth. And after my skin has been destroyed, yet in my flesh I will see God. I myself, and not another — How my heart yearns within me!"
JOB 19:25-27

CONTENTS

Acknowledgements

Ruth Hardison—My wife of 27 years, Ruth carefully read each rough draft, revision, and revised version of this manuscript. Her help and suggestions were more important to me than I can put into words. I also wish to thank her for letting me feel free to work on these materials, even when there were other things to be done.

Shirley Hansen—Words are her specialty—oh, how she can put them together! Patience, I believe, should have been her name, for she was willing to take on my ugliest attempts at writing and mold them into something beautiful and meaningful. After she edits and proofreads my work, I always want to go back and read it again and again. I thank her for countless hours spent proofreading and editing, and for her helpful suggestions that showed me how to proceed. Without her help this book would never have seen the light of day.

Pastor Kevin Westra—Pastor of Redeemer Lutheran Church of Yakima, Washington. He read my material, allowed me to bounce ideas off of him, and gave me valued counsel and encouragement.

Farrel Romig—A close friend for over 30 years. One evening while we were resting in our elk-hunting camp, he helped me work out the wording for three of the stories I consider among my very best.

Carol Romig—An elementary school teacher for 30 years, she gave of her time to proofread and suggest changes for a number of devotions.

Members of Redeemer Lutheran Church—With their wonderful Christian attitude, their willingness to be involved, and their positive comments, they have encouraged me, over the past five years, to keep on writing.

Maxine Merry—She probably didn't know what she was getting into when she said she would proofread my book, but her help and advice proved quite valuable.

Gail Thornton—The rancher in many of the stories, he and his wife, Dona, gave a lot of encouragement along the way. Gail is a dedicated Christian, who receives his inspiration from Christ and who stands as a model of inspiration for the rest of us. May he continue to "sing in the morning" for years to come.

Jan Hardison Brown—to whom I am very grateful. Although she is extremely busy, she took time to read and offer suggestions for several key articles.

Many others—friends, pastors, and relatives, who provided ideas, comments, corrections, and encouragement.

To all of these, I am very grateful.

INTRODUCTION

The following pages offer a variety of thought-provoking anecdotes about life as a Christian in today's world. If you are looking for a book on theology, you have the wrong book. However, if you are seeking a full meal of food for Christian thought, you will find it included in these pages. Some of the stories were fun to relive and write about. Others were emotionally draining. Even now, I have difficulty reading some sections without choking up because they stir up memories of emotionally charged events from my past and they speak of people who are special to me. All the events I've included in these pages really happened, either to me or to those I have known during my 60-plus years on earth. And all point to insights I have gained about my relationship with God.

These pages were written at all hours of the day and night over a period of about five years. Sometimes the thoughts came so easily I almost felt as if I were merely an instrument writing down words and phrases. At other times the page remained stubbornly empty. Only after hours of blood, sweat, tears, and prayer would someone do or say something that sparked an idea. To those people who helped get me started again, I am grateful.

While most of the material in this book is new, several of the stories appeared in another version in my first book, *The President's Corner*. Even if you have read that book, I believe you will find those selections worth another look. While my first book was written primarily for members of my home church, Redeemer Evangelical Lutheran Church in Yakima, Washington, this book is aimed at a much broader audience. In this new collection, I have tried to reach out to Christians everywhere with positive, practical anecdotes that might give them reason to meditate on their daily lives under Christ. I pray that you will join this former school teacher and part-time cowboy for a short trail ride through the mountains of life and that God will bless us as we reflect on his handiwork in our lives.

If this book causes you to rethink or reexamine your life as a follower of Christ, then I have accomplished my purpose. If, in fact, the Holy Spirit uses this book to draw you closer to himself so that your life may bear the imprint of Christ, my prayers have been answered in full.

John R. Hardison

LONELY

The fog ebbed and flowed along the ridges in front of me, while a cold wind soughed through the scrub trees behind my makeshift bench. I leaned against an old, dead snag and glassed the ridges for signs of elk. From the valley below, the forlorn howl of a lone coyote rose until it seemed that there were ten coyotes rather than one. On the hill across from me, an elk cow moved out into the open, browsing on buck brush. Standing out clearly against the early morning's skiff of snow, she regularly checked for danger as she pursued her quest for food. An occasional falling rock punctuated the sounds of the wild. Loosened by the action of freezing water and released by the warmth of the morning sun, these pieces of shale found a resting place farther down a talus slope.

It was a cool fall morning in the William O. Douglas Wilderness Area. Snow-covered mountain peaks towered above the blankets of fog. The morning sun gave them a surrealistic glow, which I knew from experience would fade as the morning became midday. Though I had dressed for the weather, my body was chilled after sitting still for a couple of hours. My toes and fingers were beginning to stiffen, and my face was cold. But it wasn't the cold that occupied my thoughts.

On this particular morning I was thinking, *Lonely.* Intellectually I knew that my hunting partner would soon be coming back from his morning hunt. I knew that the horses were only a half-mile away, and our camp, only a couple of miles farther. I also knew that my wife and home were not all that far away. But I began to think, *Lonely*.

A question about God came to my mind: *Is he here with me?* I looked around at his handiwork: the majesty of the snow-capped mountains, the gentleness of the feeding elk, the beauty of the fresh snow, and the wonder of the drifting fog. I was struck by the irony. God's handiwork is everywhere, yet so often we forget his presence. He is seen, but unseen; heard, but unheard.

Then it came to me. God was there when I started thinking, *Lonely*. He had been there all the time. My question should not have been, Is God here? but rather, Why don't I recognize God's presence?

Next time you find yourself thinking *lonely*, remember the words of the psalmist, "In my anguish I cried to the LORD, and he answered by setting me free. The LORD is with me; I will not be afraid" (Psalm 118:5,6). What a wonderful reassuring promise.

THE RIDE

Three of us had unloaded our horses along the banks of the Tieton River. After finding what remained of an abandoned road, we wound our way toward the top of a ridge a mile or two above us. The road was so overgrown with brush that in places we were forced to ride single file around low, overhanging branches. In other spots it was washed out entirely, which caused us to create some unique detours through thick, steep, rough terrain. This was a great place to try out my new horse.

At one spot the road crossed a bridge spanning the Tieton Canal. Pretty humble by most standards, the bridge consisted of two 18-inch planks laid over some four-by-fours, which rested, in turn, on a couple of large beams spanning the 10- or 12-foot crossing. One could see the rushing water between the four-by-fours. In fact, the four-by-fours were spaced just far enough apart for a horse to slip a hoof through if he stepped off the 18-inch plank. As we approached the crossing, our leader acknowledged that the bridge could be a little tricky—a fact he had neglected to mention up to that point. In any case, I didn't give my new horse any time to consider the crossing. He hesitated when he saw the rushing water, but a sharp kick in the ribs kept him from the certain disaster a midstream direction change would have caused.

Once safely on the other side, we began looking for cows to push to summer pastures above Rimrock Lake. As we gained elevation, we were greeted by a beautiful view of meadows, pine-covered ridges, cliffs, and the river and highway far below.

We finally found the cows near the top of a ridge. The trick for the leader and me was to gather the cows and herd them for half a mile down a steep, narrow trail. Then we would push them along the Tieton Canal until the cows were well on their way to the higher pastures farther up the valley. That was the task—keep those cows headed along the trails without letting the horses slip and fall in the process. While we did that, the third member of our group would ride back to the truck and bring the horse trailer up the main highway to meet us at Trout Lodge.

I had been down that trail once before, but somehow it looked steeper as my new horse slipped and slid his way down. In a few places, discretion gave way to valor as I slid down the path ahead of my horse hoping to move fast enough to get out of his way.

Around noon we came to a little pine-covered flat over-looking the river and highway with Trout Lodge nestled far below. We stopped there for lunch. It was a beautiful day with blue sky, a slight breeze, and a view few people ever get to see. It seemed as if God had given an extra stroke of his creative brush to these mountains. Because this was the last year my friend would run cattle in these hills, we rested longer than usual over lunch and conversation before pushing those cows the rest of the way. Somehow it seemed appropriate.

The life of a Christian is like that ride. It has its ups and its downs, as well as winding trails and times of seeking and finding. One has to "cowboy up" on occasion, trusting in God to get you across some of the bridges, through the detours, and down the vertical slides of life without injury. Then too, it is so important to pause at the high, pine-covered meadows and reflect with fellow Christians on the path you have followed so far. From that vantage point, it's possible to admire the beauty of God's handiwork as displayed in your life, knowing that you may not pass this way again.

"May the words of my mouth and the meditation of my heart be pleasing in your sight, O LORD, my Rock and my Redeemer" (Psalm 19:14).

A Breath of Fresh Air

My wife and I had spent most of the day balancing the checkbook, paying the monthly bills, and trying to squeeze our financial picture into the framework of our budget. It wasn't working very well. The bank statement had been difficult to reconcile; one check had not been recorded. A couple of unexpected bills had come in. We ran out of stamps. Several phone calls interrupted our work. And, because I had transposed two numbers in paying a credit card bill, we were assessed a large service charge—something I detest. Then we found a basic mistake in our budget, which meant we had to adjust the entire budget once again. In short, the day was not going well. About the middle of the afternoon, Ruth said, "I'm going outside for a breath of fresh air."

Have you ever had one of those days when you feel half dead and very discouraged by the middle of the afternoon? Your mind wanders someplace miles away. Concentrating on the task at hand seems impossible, and everything you try to do appears to fall apart. Everyone has such times. Those are times to step outside, grab a breath of fresh air, and talk with God. A little walk with God for a breath of fresh air allows us to return to work with a whole different outlook. It is just what we need to refresh our attitudes and minds.

What if it's not practical to go out for an actual walk? One of the best ways to get a breath of fresh air is to use our break time for a walk through God's Word. There we find so many passages that give us cause to be refreshed. In Philippians 4:6,7, Paul says: "Do not be anxious about anything, but in everything, by prayer and petition, with thanksgiving, present your requests to God. And the peace of God, which transcends all understanding, will guard your hearts and your minds in Christ Jesus." What a wonderful promise! We can stop what we are doing, take a short break, and walk with Jesus through his Word and prayer. We can get the needed breath of fresh air and never leave our homes, places of work, or cars.

In Psalm 17:6,7, David wrote: "I call on you, O God, for you will answer me; give ear to me and hear my prayer. Show the wonder of your great love, you who save by your right hand those who take refuge in you from their foes." Notice David uses the word *will* when he talks about God answering prayer. He doesn't say *maybe* or *sometimes*; he says, "You will answer me." How comforting is the promise that God "will" hear our prayers and give us "refuge" in our times of need.

Next time things aren't going right and you need a breath of fresh air, take a walk with Jesus. Go out and walk through God's handiwork, breathing in its beauty. Reach out your hand in prayer. Most important of all, open your Bible and listen to his promises. God will provide exactly the breath of fresh air you need.

WHOSE WILL BE DONE?

Some years ago while I was struggling to find answers and direction in my own life, I wrote the following verses. I offer them as "food for thought."

A Question of Will

Wind and snow blow cold and chill
Upon three trees on a barren height.
Answer, my soul; what moves my will?
Tall spires show radiant beauty in white,
While sleep loses to memories in the night.
Wind and snow blow cold and chill.
Rivers of living water flow from the light,
But sleep again escapes through the night.
Answer, my soul; what moves my will?
The serpent moves deeper to warmer earth,
Since to good and evil the tree's fruit gave birth.
Wind and snow blow cold and chill
As heaven and earth vie for control.
Death, life, loss, desire surround that knoll.
Answer, my soul; what moves my will?
Doubts along the way descend like snow.
Does a path through the glass darkly show?
Wind and snow blow cold and chill.
Answer, my soul; what moves my will?

God has answers for all our problems. The answers are found in his Word as we come to him in prayer. Though the glass is still dark, may God help us to see more clearly the path he would have us take each day.

"Now we see but a poor reflection as in a mirror; then we shall see face to face. Now I know in part; then I shall know fully" (1 Corinthians 13:12).

"THERE IS NO GOD!"

I got up at 5:30 A.M. to change the sprinklers so they would get a full 12-hour run before the water went back to the neighbor's place. The air was cool and crisp despite the fact that it was the first day of July. As I walked outside and began breaking down the sprinkler line, my mind wandered back to a conversation I had had with a friend years before. "There is no God," he had said. "There is no proof that there is, was, or ever will be one."

I looked around. The grass was knee high in some places. That meant my wife and I had to cut swaths with the lawn tractor so the sprinklers wouldn't get caught in the grass. I looked back at the barn. Charlie, our old black-and-white cat, yawned and stood up. He lazily crawled down off the hay bales that glistened under the sweeping rays of the early morning sun.

Having finished with the main sprinkler line, I headed back toward the other side of the house where a couple of individual units waited to be moved. The wild elms appeared green and healthy, and a light breeze rustled their leaves; the weeping willows seemed to sway in unison. As I continued my work, the sun again peeked through the broken clouds, trimming them with shades of silver and gold. Now and then, from the valley, I could hear the sound of a car. Somewhere, far away, a rooster sounded his wake-up call.

As I finished setting the corner sprinkler, I looked back toward the kitchen. The pines and firs we had planted so many years before now nearly blocked my view. I stopped, taking in their beauty. Each branch sported new growth, which glistened in the sun—shining fingers pointing toward the heavens.

My old friend's words came back to me again: "There is no God." I looked around once more and smiled.

As I headed back to the house, I thought, *There is no God? If my friend ever got up early on a cool summer morning, he must have never opened his eyes.*

"The heavens declare the glory of God; the skies proclaim the work of his hands" (Psalm 19:1). "The heavens are yours, and yours also the earth; you founded the world and all that is in it" (Psalm 89:11).

HOWDY, PARTNER

In a newspaper cartoon, a father was observing his little boy, dressed as a cowboy, as he knelt by his bed saying his prayers. The father asked the little guy something like, "Do you always start your prayers with 'Howdy, Partner'?" As I read the cartoon, I couldn't help but smile.

Later, the image of the little boy, kneeling in prayer and addressing God as "Partner," kept buzzing around in my head. The cartoon was cute, but it also seemed to highlight a truth I had overlooked. When we pray, we come as we are. Does it matter whether we are a housewife, farmer, businessman, pastor, or a small child dressed as a cowboy? Does it matter if we say "Lord" or "Partner" when we address God in prayer, as long as we do it reverently? Here was a child, a fictional child to be sure, but a child, communicating with God in a way that made sense to him at that particular moment in his young life. The longer I thought about that cartoon, the more I realized how blessed we are that we can come to God in prayer at any time and in any place. More important than where we are or what time it is, God wants us to pray humbly, sincerely, and often.

Prayer is one of the greatest privileges we have as Christians. And what better statement could we possibly make about our lives than to say that God is our partner?

Listen to some of the things our Lord has told us about prayer: "Therefore I tell you, whatever you ask for in prayer, believe that you have received it, and it will be yours. And when you stand praying, if you hold anything against anyone, forgive him, so that your Father in heaven may forgive you your sins" (Mark 11:24,25). "Do not be anxious about anything, but in everything, by prayer and petition, with thanksgiving, present your requests to God. And the peace of God, which transcends all understanding, will guard your hearts and your minds in Christ Jesus" (Philippians 4:6,7).

Perhaps we could learn a lesson from the kid in the cartoon and say "Howdy, Partner" to our Lord more often.

LEARNING TO BE A CHRISTIAN IS LIKE LEARNING TO SKI

Ever since 1948 when it snowed once on my folks' California ranch, I have been fascinated with skiing. I got my chance to learn while attending Whitworth College in Spokane, Washington. When a ski class was offered for a physical education credit, I quickly signed up, even though I had no equipment.

When I wrote my folks to tell them I wanted to learn to ski, they thought I was nuts. But they told me to get what I needed. I bought used leather, lace-up boots for 20 dollars; worn out wooden skis, with cable bindings I had to adjust with a nickel, for 12 dollars; poles for 3 dollars; ski pants for 20 dollars; canvas gloves for 5 dollars; and heavy wool socks for 2 dollars. For 30 dollars I got a ski coat, which I wore every day for three winters. Though I couldn't afford long johns, my flannel pajamas worked reasonably well. As part of that class back in 1960, I got six rides to the mountain, lessons, and lift tickets, all for 25 dollars. The first two days I tried to ski, I thought I was going to die. However, it gradually became easier, and I was hooked for life.

For many people, myself included, becoming a new Christian is like starting to ski. In my childhood, I had some interest in the biblical stories. My folks gave me the opportunity to attend church and provided me with a Bible. The materials didn't cost much: a few workbooks for Sunday school, a few trinkets for memorizing verses, and some ribbons or pins for good attendance. I did take a few interesting trips and outings with church groups. What helped most to develop a desire to learn more was the encouragement from my Sunday school teachers and my parents. Eventually, I wanted to learn more.

As with skiing, there have been times in my life when I felt I was doing well as a Christian, times when I had my doubts, and times when I lost much of my interest.

After graduating from college, I came to Yakima, Washington, to teach at the junior high level. Skiing was not something my wife and I could afford, either money- or time-wise. Our son was little, and we had no money for a baby-sitter so we could take a day off for skiing. However, we never lost the desire to ski.

One day, four or five years after coming to Yakima, we drove past the White Pass ski resort. It was a beautiful winter day, and we could see the skiers coming down the runs. That old skiing bug jumped right out and bit us again. Within a week we were at the sporting goods store buying all new equipment. It wasn't great equipment, but it was at least safer than our old stuff.

Church was like that too. There was definitely a down- time for us in the late sixties, though we never quit attending altogether. Although we had tried several churches, we never got deeply involved. Granted, it was partly our own fault—we just didn't put in as much effort and study as we should have—but those churches were never like a family to us.

After my first wife left me in 1974, I attended several other churches, looking for a place to call home. After a number of trials, my wife-to-be, Ruth, pushed me in the direction of Redeemer Lutheran Church in Yakima. Though it took me years to fully realize it, I had found my new church home.

Ruth had attended a WELS church (Wisconsin Evangelical Lutheran Synod) all her life, but she had skied little before we met. I had skied quite a bit but had never attended a WELS church. We both learned something. She got so she could ski quite well in spite of my lessons. And over the years, I became more and more involved at Redeemer and gradually grew in God's grace. Today, we are still learning what it means to be Christians and learning about skiing. With God's help, we will continue learning for the rest of our years.

Learning to ski, like growing to be a mature Christian, takes time and encouragement. If you fall, you get up and try again. Putting on the skis is just the start. So is confirmation. Most of the learning takes place afterward. If we quit there, we never get off the "bunny slope."

Give it some thought. Are you ready for the starter, intermediate, advanced, or expert slopes of life? More important, what are you doing to enable yourself to grow?

May the Lord help us each realize that confirmation day is only the start of our Christian life. May we understand the very real need to grow in our Christian faith, and may we understand that growing in faith takes a lifetime. The Lord tells us, "The seed on good soil stands for those with a noble and good heart, who hear the word, retain it, and by persevering produce a crop" (Luke 8:15). God's Word also says: "Grow in the grace and knowledge of our Lord and Savior Jesus Christ. To him be glory both now and forever! Amen" (2 Peter 3:18).

My Favorite
Bible Translation

——————•——————

I was scanning the bookcase in the dining area of our kitchen when my eyes came to the shelf containing our Bibles. There were enough Bible translations lined up all in a row to keep a person reading for months.

When I was growing up, I had used the King James Version. In my college days I studied the Revised Standard Version. Now I usually read the New International Version. However, sometimes when we really want to study a portion of the Bible from a number of different angles, my wife and I also use our copies of the Amplified New Testament, the Phillip's Translation, the Revised King James, the Good News, the Jerusalem Bible, and the Living Bible. Then too, we can call our pastor and ask him to search several other translations and even the original languages.

We believe the Bible is the inspired Word of God, without error. So why don't all these versions say exactly the same thing? Of course there are many answers to that question. The original writings were inspired and without error, but the copies were passed down by men. Unfortunately, try as they would to make perfect copies, sometimes they miscopied a letter or a word. However, the minor differences that resulted didn't affect any doctrine or teaching of Scripture. Also, sometimes it's challenging to express the precise meaning of an ancient language in modern English. The ancients occasionally used words that have no exact equivalent today. Or some words can mean several different things in English. There are even a couple of words for which we have no definitions.

Is that something we should be concerned about? Actually, no. When we think about it, it is really remarkable the way God has preserved his Word down through the ages. The message of the Bible comes through no matter which translation is used. Some versions may say it more clearly or more poetically, but the messages of law and gospel come through in all of them.

So what is my favorite translation? Over the years, my favorite—the one that gets the message across the best for me—is the one I see written in the lives of my strong Christian friends. I don't know which written translation they used to get God's message. Nor do I care. For me, the point is that they got it. The Holy Spirit used the Word to change their hearts; I see God's Word clearly demonstrated in their everyday lives. Their lives exemplify the truth: Actions speak louder than words.

We call ourselves Christians, sinners who were made God's own by the blood of Christ. That means we are Christ's ambassadors—we represent Christ. Our lives are living translations of his Word. Every time we open our mouths to speak or we react to what others are doing or saying, we are open books that others can read. That thought challenges us to consider the message others will read when they look at our "translation" of God's Word.

Jesus said it best: "You are the light of the world. A city on a hill cannot be hidden. Neither do people light a lamp and put it under a bowl. Instead they put it on its stand, and it gives light to everyone in the house. In the same way, let your light shine before men, that they may see your good deeds and praise your Father in heaven" (Matthew 5:14-16).

DEALING WITH DEPRESSION

Christians are not exempt from depression. In our stressed-out world, many Christian folks struggle with it. Studies show that many pastors are on the brink of burnout. As a result, many may end up leaving the ministry. With all our modern conveniences, living is supposed to be so much easier for us than for our ancestors. Yet families break up in record numbers, young people wander with no sense of direction, and many people long for a different life, in a different place, doing something different.

Why so much dissatisfaction? We Christians search for answers to that question as much as anyone else. But we have an advantage. We can share our hurts and our frustrations with God in prayer. And in his Word, we have something we can hang on to when the world seems to be spinning out of control. We are not alone in our fight against the pressures of life. We are not left to climb out of the pit of depression by ourselves.

In the mid-seventies, my life was turned upside down. My father, grandfather, and a close friend from college all died within a few months of one another. My maternal grandfather became terminally ill. In the middle of all that, my wife left me to marry a person I had once considered a close friend. I still had my son, but there were continuing debates over custody. Those were not easy times, but God was there to hold me up, and even to bless me.

Ruth was one of God's greatest blessings. About a year after my first wife left, Ruth and I began dating; a few months later, we were married. Ruth was a more mature Christian than I. She helped me through some pretty rough times.

During this difficult period, I wrote the following poem.

Demons of the Soul

Demons that possess my soul, be gone.
Sleep eludes me, a feather in the wind.
What new phantoms can haunt me now?
The reaper has met friend and father at the bend.
One meaning much resigns, life's beauty ends.
Demons that possess my soul, be gone.
Most friends stay true, though minds are all but glad.
One impersonates Judas—I may go mad.
What new phantoms can haunt me now?
Can my mind be lucid? awake?
A dark, serpentine line awaits another at the gate.
Demons that possess my soul, be gone.
New blood flows through a family of defeat.
The son remains, trees of life sprout like wheat.
What new phantoms can haunt me now?
Lawyers discuss with innuendoes and half-truths.
Will the son fade, replaced by telephone booths?
Demons that possess my soul, be gone.
What new phantoms can haunt me now?

Depression is an ugly world that exists beyond the borders of sadness. Everyone is sad from time to time, but deep depression seems to have no exit. It reminds me of a deep, brick-lined well—an old-fashioned well with a bucket hanging from a rope. In my mind's eye, it is circular, about 10 feet across. Sinking into depression is like descending into that well. At first the brick-lined sides offer some handholds, perhaps happy memories, helpful friends, or a special Bible verse. However, the deeper one descends, the fewer the handholds and the slicker the walls. At first you struggle as hard as you can to climb out, but eventually you lose your will and begin to free-fall. If allowed to go unchecked, the descent into the well of depression will ultimately lead to total darkness, defeat, feelings of hopelessness, and perhaps death.

God helped me by sending wonderful Christian people, not the least of whom was Ruth. Eventually with God's help, they were able to send down a bucket made of love and to pull me out of that dark well of depression. I couldn't have gotten out or stayed out on my own. But the world looks better when lit by the encouraging sunshine of my Christian wife and friends—a lot better.

Addressing the problems that continue to invade our lives before they get out of hand is paramount. I can't stress enough how important it is that we hear the Word of God, both in church and Bible class, and that we talk to God in prayer. How much easier it might have been if I had just been better versed in the Word of God. The answers—the comfort and hope—are there.

Here are a few passages I have found helpful when faced with overwhelming problems and possible depression:

- "You are a shield around me, O LORD; you bestow glory on me and lift up my head. To the LORD I cry aloud, and he answers me from his holy hill. I lie down and sleep; I wake again, because the LORD sustains me. I will not fear the tens of thousands drawn up against me on every side" (Psalm 3:3-6).

- "We wait in hope for the LORD; he is our help and our shield. In him our hearts rejoice, for we trust in his holy name" (Psalm 33:20,21).

- "Why are you downcast, O my soul? Why so disturbed within me? Put your hope in God, for I will yet praise him, my Savior and my God" (Psalm 42:11).

- "He heals the brokenhearted and binds up their wounds" (Psalm 147:3).

- "Great is our Lord and mighty in power; his understanding has no limit" (Psalm 147:5).

PROMISES MADE,
PROMISES KEPT

The other day the sun shown through the window onto my Bible. That got me thinking about all the wonderful promises God has made. A few examples came to mind. "Be strong and courageous. Do not be afraid or terrified because of them, for the LORD your God goes with you; he will never leave you nor forsake you" (Deuteronomy 31:6). "So do not fear, for I am with you; do not be dismayed, for I am your God. I will strengthen you and help you; I will uphold you with my righteous right hand" (Isaiah 41:10). "Let us not become weary in doing good, for at the proper time we will reap a harvest if we do not give up" (Galatians 6:9). "I can do everything through him who gives me strength" (Philippians 4:13).

Over the years, I have drawn strength from those promises in many different settings.

I remembered those promises on one of the most wonderful, sunny days I have ever experienced. Blue skies held only wisps of clouds that were pushed by a gentle breeze. Wildflowers filled the green meadows as far as the eye could see. The beauty and grandeur of the Canadian Rockies towering in the distance caused us to pause in quiet contemplation. Butterflies floated from flower to flower. Hoary marmots stood upright, whistling warnings of our approach as we walked along a winding mountain path. Streams flowed peacefully through the flat meadows, roared down steep rocky beds, and occasionally fell away from the earth's grasp to form some unnamed waterfall.

The entire day had been an example of the goodness of God's promises.

I remembered those promises also on that Sunday morning, May 18, 1980. The day had been beautiful and bright when we walked into church in Yakima, Washington. But from 9:30 to 10:30, as Ruth and I worshiped, a shroud of darkness slipped over us from the west. I kept thinking, *This must be one gigantic thunderstorm.*

By the end of the service, darkness totally engulfed the church—it was as dark as night outside. As we sang the final hymn, Pastor stepped outside. When he came back to give the closing announcements, he had a strange look on his face. He reported that Mount Saint Helens must have erupted because ash was falling like rain outside.

That was a day like none other. When we finally got home, it was pitch black at midday. We looked out our windows. No stars. No moon. No lights in the valley. No lights in the neighbors' houses. Absolute black was all that met our eyes. It was even more eerie because of the repeated thunderclaps that shook our house to its very foundation.

God's promises were important that day.

I remember yet another clear summer day in the mountains. Ruth and I had accompanied a class of 16 adults to look at the remnants of a petrified forest northeast of Roosevelt Lodge in Yellowstone Park. It took about two hours to climb to our vantage point high on the ridge above the highway. As we looked across the petrified trees to the north, we noticed threatening clouds and heard the unmistakable rumble of approaching thunder. We could see that the storm would be upon us in minutes.

Deciding that discretion was the better part of valor, we began zigzagging our way down the hillside toward the safety of our vehicles. We had gone only a short distance when we noticed a couple who were still working their way to the top of the ridge in spite of the approaching lightning.

In order to determine how close the lightning was, we counted the seconds between a lightning flash and its corresponding thunderclap. About five seconds means about one mile. Suddenly our leader stopped counting and shouted, "Get down!"

We knelt just as lightning hit the tree, only 75 feet away, where the two hikers had taken shelter. The lightning bolt traveled down the tree and struck the two people, throwing them off their feet and shredding their clothes. The lady ended up wedged between two smaller trees. The man stopped rolling about 40 feet down the hill. When we got to them, neither was breathing. Fortunately we had a radio to call for a rescue helicopter. Fortunately also, one person in our group was a CPR instructor and several others had received training. But practicing CPR on a flat surface indoors doesn't prepare a person for what we faced. Lightning bolts were striking all around us, and the wet, foot-high grass made the steep hillside as slick as grease. People had to crouch on the downhill side to hold each injured person in place while others took turns doing CPR. There were more than a few of us praying as we worked on them for the hour it took the helicopter to arrive. Amazingly the people survived, though they suffered blown eardrums and nasty burns, and they had no memory of ever being in the park.

God's promises were good that day too. *Yes,* I thought to myself, *God's promises are always good, bringing wonderful assurance and peace to us no matter what our circumstances.*

May God help us all to take more time to study and learn about his promises. May he strengthen our faith so that we always believe those promises.

———•———

ORDINARY PEOPLE DO EXTRAORDINARY WORK

God's work isn't reserved only for extraordinary people with extraordinary skills. His work is done by ordinary people who are willing to use ordinary skills to God's glory. Sometimes we mumble, "I would like to help, but I just can't." Why do we say such things? Look at Moses. He was hesitant, inarticulate, reluctant—but God used him for great things. In fact, the Bible is full of examples of how God used very ordinary people—fishermen, shepherds, a carpenter, a peasant girl—to do his will.

To do our work today, we depend upon all sorts of technology: e-mail, computers, TVs, mass media, the Internet, cordless phones, cellular phones, and a host of machinery and tools. God, however, still does his work through human hands and voices. We witness by example. We invite. We pray. We volunteer. We tell others what we know. This is our privilege and our sacred duty to our Lord. But it is not our wisdom or skill that accomplishes anything. It is purely by God's grace that we have the privilege to serve.

In 1 Corinthians 1:26, Paul instructs us: "Think of what you were when you were called. Not many of you were wise by human standards; not many were influential; not many were of noble birth." Does God really use us with all our faults and weaknesses? Yes! Yes! Yes!

But what can we do? Actually, whenever we use our lives to give honor to God, he can accomplish important things through our work. We can:

- set an example for others by being in church and Bible study
- bring our kids to Sunday school
- participate in special programs
- attend church functions and invite others
- sing in the choir or play an instrument
- pray and serve on a prayer chain
- serve on committees and in church offices
- bring food for the various dinners and help wash dishes
- help with mailings and read the church newsletter
- visit the sick and provide rides to church
- compliment others honestly when they have done a good job
- assist with Sunday school
- set up for special functions and usher
- donate extra dollars
- study our Bibles and have daily meditations
- clean the church and help with repairs
- put up decorations, bring flowers, or make banners
- share a religious book
- greet guests who come to church—and ask them back
- surprise others with gifts that remind them of the Lord
- talk to others about the grace of God that is the focus of our church

The more we do these things, the more we will find we are able to do. And God will bless the kingdom through our work.

Yes, God works through ordinary people to do extraordinary work. Let's make a list of all the talents and gifts we have for doing his work. And let's get busy, remembering that we have every reason to offer God the best of our time, talents, and treasures. "For Christ's love compels us, because we are convinced that...he died for all, that those who live should no longer live for themselves but for him who died for them and was raised again" (2 Corinthians 5:14,15).

WIMPY—A PARABLE

One cold spring day, we arrived home from work to find that our Norwegian elkhound had given birth to her first litter. Of the three pups, only one tiny puppy was still alive. We quickly bundled him up and fixed a nice bed for him in the garage. Though the puppy did get older, it's hard to say that he actually grew up. When he was full grown, he stood only about a third of the height of his mother. Because he was such a runt, we called him Wimpy.

Wimpy loved to ride in my son's red wagon. He would stand "tall" with his tail in the air as Greg hauled him all around the yard and up and down the road near our home.

Wimpy had a great disposition, and we loved him. He became a member of our family just as a person becomes a member of a church family. He took part in all the activities. Always ready to get involved, he was the first in line for something new. He greeted everyone who came to the house. He ate the food we put in front of him. And though he didn't grow tall, he did grow healthy and stout. He could stand his own against most any other dog who dared question him. All in all, he was a great asset to our family.

Then one summer day in July, my son was killed in an accident. When Ruth and I arrived home, Wimpy was sitting on the front porch looking lost. There would be no more romps in the fields with Greg. No more rides in the red wagon as Greg pulled it down the street with a rope attached to his bike. No more following Greg as he explored the countryside on horseback.

Seven months later, Ruth and I moved to a new house on a ridge a couple of miles to the south. Wimpy seemed to adjust to his new home; there were fields to explore and new dogs to meet. Actually, Wimpy was already pretty well known in the area because he had always followed when we rode our horses throughout the surrounding country.

After a few months, however, he started disappearing for days at a time. When we did see him, he seemed to be the same old Wimpy. He would wag his tail, share our food, and have fellowship with us. But then he would disappear again for longer and longer periods of time.

One day the lady who cleaned house for us saw a strange-looking animal all covered in dirt and blood. It was Wimpy, but he had been so beaten and torn by some unknown enemy, she didn't recognize him. When we got home, he looked up at us as if to say, "Help me just one more time!" We did. It took weeks, including a trip to the veterinarian, a bunch of stitches, doses of medicine, and daily feedings. At the end of that time, Wimpy's health was back on track. Once again he spent time with our family and participated in all our activities. No one ever questioned whether we would take him back into the fold. We had missed him greatly. And he seemed happy to be back.

About four months later, we took a two-week trip to California to visit my mother. Neighbors were to feed Wimpy and our other animals while we were gone. But when we came home, Wimpy was nowhere to be found. The people who had done the chores said that one day he just wasn't there. We searched for him, calling his name each morning and evening, hoping that he would once again come back to the family that loved him. He never returned.

Though it has been many years, a feeling of emptiness still throbs in our hearts. Just the other day, I asked Ruth when she thought Wimpy might come back to be a part of our family and eat our food once again.

Would we welcome him? You bet! Would it matter where he had been or what he had done? Not a bit! Would we still extend our love to him? More than ever!

Is there a message in this story? I hope so. Think about the members of our churches whom we haven't seen in a while. And think about Jesus' words: "Whoever comes to me I will never drive away" (John 6:37) and "My Father's will is that everyone who looks to the Son and believes in him shall have eternal life" (John 6:40).

The church doors are always open, and we continue to keep watch—ready to welcome missing family members back into the fold. Let us continue to pray that God will touch the hearts of our brothers and sisters who are missing from God's house and that through his Holy Spirit, he will guide them back to his home.

DO YOU SING
IN THE MORNING?

My day started with physical therapy for some back and leg problems. Then I accompanied a friend on his rounds as he fed his cattle at the far east end of the Yakima valley. It was a dark, wet, snowy day. By the time we stopped for lunch, we were covered with soggy hay stalks and chaff. Next we stopped at the Big R for oil, extension cords, light-bulbs, and a few other supplies. On the way back to the ranch, we stopped at the church to haul last year's Christmas trees to the burn pile.

That's not what most people would call a thrilling day, but for me it was very relaxing. I had a chance to talk to my friend about a whole bunch of things. He always seemed interested, and he had good common-sense advice that made me feel better about my problems. Because I had been given a larger-than-usual set of problems during the previous weeks, I needed a chance to relax.

When we got to his house, he invited me to stay and watch a video that showed segments of Elvis singing gospel songs, old rock-and-roll stars singing their hits, and sons and daughters of country singers performing the songs that had made their parents famous. He used the fast forward button liberally to get to the sections that were the high-lights of those shows. After listening for a while from the kitchen, his wife came in and joined us.

As he waited for the tape to rewind, he walked into the

other room singing one of the tunes we had just heard. His wife looked at me and asked, "Do you sing in the morning?" Her question caught me totally off guard. I love to sing, but I instinctively knew that wasn't the real point of her question.

I answered with a weak "No," to which she replied, "Well, he always does. He is just a happy person!"

I thought about her comment for a good part of that evening. Why was it fun to spend time with this person doing mundane things on an otherwise dreary day? What made the difference?

Then it hit me! He was a happy person. He brought sunshine and a song to the lives of those who knew him, especially his wife. What a wonderful compliment his wife had paid him! Here was a person who was happy and at peace with himself and his Lord. What better testimony could any Christian give?

In James 5:13 it says, "Is any one of you in trouble? He should pray. Is anyone happy? Let him sing songs of praise." I have thought about that verse a lot. The Lord is with us and will stay with us through all our challenges, so shouldn't we all "sing in the morning"? If we all focused on the good things God has done for us and reflected our thanks all through our lives, what a difference we could make for others! What a testimony our lives would be!

I made up my mind that with the Lord's help, my life would be an expression of God's goodness. Then maybe I can sing in the morning. Better yet, perhaps I can help someone else want to sing in the morning too.

IT WASN'T MY TIME

In Deuteronomy 31:6, we read these comforting words: "The LORD your God goes with you; he will never leave you nor forsake you." This is a promise I have come to believe. God is with us no matter where we may be. He is with us to carry out his plan for us in our lives.

Yes, God has a plan for us. Though it is a good plan, we don't know all the details. Nor do we know when God's plan for us on earth will end. That question about when our time on earth will end, often comes to mind, particularly when a person walks away from a serious incident that so easily could have ended in death.

Have you ever heard someone say "I should have been killed; it just wasn't my time"? There have been times in my life when, for some unknown reason, God chose to allow my wife and me to walk away from a potentially deadly accident. The Lord was watching over us, just as he watches over everyone.

Once during my high school years, I was approaching a familiar country intersection on my way home from church when I felt I needed to slow down. For a teenager to slow down on a straight road was unusual to say the least. Yet, because the feeling kept getting stronger, I slowed to under 20 miles an hour. Just before I reached the intersection, a car ran the stop sign. Squealing around the corner on two wheels, it barely missed the front of my car.

Another time, I was on my way to the movies with my girlfriend. I was driving the speed limit when a car passed me. We were looking at something along the road when I suddenly realized that the car that had passed only a moment before had stopped to pick up a hitchhiker. Because the hitchhiker was standing beside the road and another car was approaching in the opposite lane, all I could do was hit the brakes. We slid for about a hundred feet before we slammed into the stopped car. The car's occupants, the hitchhiker, and I were unhurt. My girlfriend suffered a relatively minor bump on her head. My car, however, was a mess. In California you virtually always get a ticket if you hit another car in the rear. Though I had to pay to repair my own car, I didn't get a ticket.

A few years ago I was driving home from work when I noticed a car coming from the other direction at about 40 miles an hour. I barely had time to slow down as the oncoming car drifted into my lane and hit the car ahead of me. Then, as if in slow motion, the colliding car careened on two wheels toward me. It almost turned over but finally righted itself and stopped just a few feet in front of my car. Had it rolled over, I could have been killed. As it was, I didn't have a scratch—nor did my car.

Shortly after that incident, Ruth and I were on the way to work in our old GMC truck. I was traveling about 35 miles an hour when I hit a patch of black ice and began to slide toward a school bus that was approaching in the opposite lane. I remember telling Ruth, "Hold on! I am going to dump this truck rather than hit that bus." I turned the wheel into a hard skid. The truck spun nearly 360 degrees without turning over, leaving the pavement, or hitting anything. By rights, on such a narrow road, our vehicle should have been through the barbed wire fence and on its side in the pasture.

Another time, Ruth fell asleep while she was driving home. Only inches from driving off the shoulder of the road, she clipped a mailbox with the mirror. The impact jarred her awake and saved her from serious injury or even death.

Just a few winters ago, I was driving slower than usual on my way home. Suddenly an approaching white pickup hit a patch of ice and slid sideways into my lane. Had I been going my usual speed, he would have smashed the driver's side of my car.

I could tell of other near misses. Once I was almost shot while hunting. Another time I nearly fell down a rock slide that ended with a drop-off of several hundred feet. Still another time, my horse reared over backward on top of me. The saddle horn stabbed the ground only inches from my side.

Where was God in all of this? According to the Bible, he was right there by my side. Some people die in similar situations; some walk away. We don't know all the reasons why, but we do know God has a plan for each of us. "There is a time for everything, and a season for every activity under heaven: a time to be born and a time to die" (Ecclesiastes 3:1,2). To be hurt or killed on those particular days was not part of God's plan for us. It was not "our time" to die.

Everyone will die someday. Some will die sooner than our human understanding believes they should. However, God knows the span of time every life will cover. With the psalmist, we acknowledge, "My times are in [God's] hands" (Psalm 31:15). And we know that his plan for our lives, however long they may be, is good. "'I know the plans I have for you,' declares the LORD, 'plans to prosper you and not to harm you, plans to give you hope and a future'" (Jeremiah 29:11). Our job is not to worry about when our time on earth is up. Rather, we are to concern ourselves with the things God wants us to accomplish while we're here.

Let's begin each day with a prayer that the Holy Spirit will keep us safely on the path God wants us to follow until it is "our time." Let us live each day as though it is our last opportunity to give glory to God here on earth. It may be.

———— • ————

MY BUCKET HAS
A HOLE IN IT!

Sometimes my faith is like a bucket with a hole in it! I know. Some people suggest that my faith must be strong: I have held a variety of offices in the church, I attend services regularly, I go to all the meetings and most of the church functions. I'm a Sunday morning greeter, and I even write a column for the newsletter. So they think my faith must be strong. I wish I could make that claim. I can't. My bucket of faith has a hole in it.

Sometimes, when things don't go right, that bucket leaks so badly it is difficult to keep going! At times I feel like crawling into a hole to forget all the things that are going wrong in my life.

At times I am convinced I have more than my fair share of frustrations, questions, and problems. That's especially when I have to stop and refill my bucket. I do that by turning to the Scriptures and reading passages like "With joy you will draw water from the wells of salvation" (Isaiah 12:3) or "The LORD is my strength and my song; he has become my salvation" (Exodus 15:2).

How thankful we can be that Isaiah was right, that we can "draw water from the wells of salvation"! Since most of us have some pretty fair holes in our buckets, let us be thankful also that we are allowed more than one bucketful of faith.

"Give thanks to the LORD, call on his name; make known among the nations what he has done, and proclaim that his name is exalted. Sing to the LORD, for he has done glorious things; let this be known to all the world. Shout aloud and sing for joy, . . . for great is the Holy One of Israel among you" (Isaiah 12:4-6).

CHRISTIAN LOVE MAKES ALL THE DIFFERENCE

I had just gotten home one cold December day when the phone rang. As Ruth handed the phone to me, I could tell something wasn't right. At the other end of the line, my brother spoke quietly. "There is no easy way to say this. Uncle Bernard had a heart attack this morning. He didn't make it. I felt I should let you know right away. I know the two of you were close."

About 15 years my senior, Bernard was like an older brother to me. We often rode our horses together in the back country. From the time I was a little kid, we had hunted together. I can even remember hunting deer with him when I was too young to carry a gun. One time we spotted a big buck across a canyon. Bernard spent a good couple of minutes getting a good rest on a boulder before he was ready to take a shot. Being young and impatient, I finally said, "Just when are you going to shoot anyhow?" He got the buck, but I never heard the end of that incident.

Bernard was also my hero. When he came home from the navy, I started wearing sailor hats. Later, when I was growing up, I would ride my horse down to his place to visit with him and his wife, Maxine.

Bernard influenced my life and my interests in a number of ways. A great Dodgers fan, he nurtured my interest in baseball by taking me to see their games in Los Angeles. He was also a Christian who was very active in his church.

He was one of the people who influenced me to get more involved in church activities.

In Bernard's and Maxine's later years, Ruth and I would visit them whenever we traveled to California to see my mother. We always picked up where we had left off the time before; he was fun to be around. The years and advanced Parkinson's disease took their toll on Uncle Bernard's health, however. The last time I visited him, he was having a tough time. But he rallied when he saw me at the door and pretended to spar with me as I walked into the room. One final time, we shared some of the old hunting stories and reminisced about old times.

On the way back to Yakima, I found a little toy figure wearing a Dodgers hat—one of those windup gizmos that did all sorts of silly antics. I wrapped it up and sent it to him. Maxine sent me a picture of him watching that toy figure with the Dodgers game on the TV in the background. I am looking at that photograph as I write this.

On that bleak December day when I heard that he had died, I was stunned. He was only in his 60s. Even though I had known he wasn't well, I had not expected him to die.

The next few days were a real down time for me. I wanted to go to California for his funeral, but job obligations made that impossible. Though I sent flowers and spoke with Maxine over the phone, I still felt down.

Though not many people in Yakima knew I had lost someone special, my pastor's wife found out. She took the time and effort to send a card with a beautiful message from Scripture and an expression of her personal sympathy over the loss of my uncle. I can't tell you how much her card meant. I have received a lot of mail since that day several years ago, but nothing more important to me than her thoughtful card. I was hurting, and it told me there was another Christian out there who cared. Her quiet

Christian act has also been a tremendous inspiration to me to use whatever gifts God has given me to serve him and his people.

"This is the message you heard from the beginning: We should love one another" (1 John 3:11). May God help us to be vigilant, watching for others who may benefit from a gesture of Christian love. May we learn to recognize what our friends, acquaintances, and coworkers need. There are plenty of opportunities to show Christian love if we just look for them. It's a wonderful way to witness our Christian faith to others.

Give it some thought. Is there someone you might help today?

THE EXAMPLE

Using God-given gifts to serve the church family starts with you. Your example may be more important to people around you than you have ever realized.

When I taught high school, I used to tell the ninth graders about the eighth graders, at the middle school across the street, who were watching them and following their example. It was true. Those eighth graders looked to the older students to see how they should act and what they should do when they became high school students.

Whether we know it or not, as members of Christ's church, we are being watched. Others notice our involvement in the life of the church—our service to the Lord of the church—and copy us. Several people in my home church in California and several in my current church in Washington have been real inspirations to me. Their selfless gifts of time, money, and talents given for their churches have inspired me to stay involved in the Lord's work. Most of the time they were unaware of their far-reaching influence. However, I learned a lot from what they did and how they gave of themselves for the good of the Lord and his church. Some of those people have passed away, but others may be reading these words, not realizing how they witnessed to me by their actions.

Think about it! Your spouse, children, fellow church members, and church visitors are looking to you and me as examples to follow. Are we in step with Christ? If our unnoticed observers do as we do, will God be praised?

"In the same way, let your light shine before men, that they may see your good deeds and praise your Father in heaven" (Matthew 5:16). May we ask the Lord to work in us each day so that our Christian light will shine as a bright beacon to show others the face of Christ.

——— • ———

THE CONNECTION

Some relatives who were visiting us had an electrical problem with their motor home. The battery would seem to go dead even while the motor home was running down the road. Each time they turned the engine off, an auxiliary battery was needed to get it started again.

We took it to a friend who is an excellent mechanic. He was able to locate the problem in only a few minutes. Though the battery connections looked good, one was actually quite corroded. The mechanic described the problem as being like a 16-strand wire with all but 2 or 3 of the strands broken. Enough electricity was getting through the few remaining strands to trickle charge the battery. This allowed the vehicle to keep running while on the road. However, when a lot of power was needed for the critical task of turning the motor over to start it, those few strands could not carry the heavy load. After the bad connection was carefully cleaned and tightened, electricity again flowed freely and the engine started easily time after time.

On the way home I thought about how that battery connection reminded me of another much more important connection: the one we have with God. Sometimes this connection gets a little corroded too. To other people, we may look fine on the outside, but underneath, things may not be what they seem. We may show up in church a majority of Sundays, perhaps even read the Bible and attend a Bible class now and then. But career concerns, health challenges, plans for the future, family problems—you name it—distract us and keep us from hearing the precious words of our Savior. As time goes on, our faith begins to weaken. We can probably continue in this fashion for weeks, months, or even years as long as things go smoothly and our faith isn't tested too much. The problem comes when something really taxes our beliefs, such as a serious illness, a divorce, a death, or any of a hundred other serious problems life can throw our way. Because of our weak connection with God, who alone is our strength, we can falter or fall altogether.

Life and the devil have a way of sending some big problems and temptations at us with little or no notice. We cannot afford to be connected to God by only a few strands. How do we stay better connected? We must make use of the tools God has given us to keep our connection with God open. The Bible calls these tools the armor of God. In Paul's letter to the Ephesians, he says: "Put on the full armor of God, so that when the day of evil comes, you may be able to stand your ground, and after you have done everything, to stand. Stand firm then, with the belt of truth buckled around your waist, with the breastplate of righteousness in place, and with your feet fitted with the readiness that comes from the gospel of peace. In addition to all this, take up the shield of faith, with which you can extinguish all the flaming arrows of the evil one. Take the helmet of salvation and the sword of the Spirit, which is the word of God. And pray in the Spirit on all occasions with all kinds of prayers and requests" (6:13-18).

Have you checked your connection to God lately? When you sit down in church, or read a devotion at home, do you ask God to quiet your heart so that you can hear him speak? Do you ask him to keep your eyes focused on the cross of Christ, which is your most important treasure, so that you aren't distracted by the worthless treasures this world offers?

Since we all let our connection with God get a little loose and corroded at times, periodic and regular checks are very important. May God help us to be vigilant and to put on the full suit of Christian armor. We just might need it today!

WHAT WILL MOMMY SAY?

When I was teaching at the junior high level, I told the story of a little kid and his rabbit drawing to show how words and actions can motivate others.

Visualize a little boy who has just opened his presents on his third birthday. Off to his bedroom he goes with his new coloring book and box of crayons. He plops down on the floor, spreads out the crayons, and opens the book. He selects a page with the outline of a large cottontail rabbit. Because he is only three, he really doesn't know what color goes where. And with his limited motor skills he isn't able to keep the colors inside the lines. But he is excited, and he wants his parents to be proud. Picking green for the nose, he colors it vigorously, going outside the outline. Red seems right for the body, blue for the feet, yellow for the ears, and purple for the head. The grass, he figures, should be pink. And so he colors with a flourish of activity.

Then it is time to show the masterpiece to Mom. With coloring book in hand, he runs out of the crayon-strewn bedroom, finds his extremely busy mom in the kitchen, and expectantly raises the colored picture for her to see.

The next few seconds are extremely important. Picture her reaction. Will she say: "I'll look at it later. I don't have time right now"? Or: "Look at that mess! The colors are all wrong, and you didn't stay inside the lines"? If she ignores or criticizes his work, the child's downcast response will show immediately on his three-year-old face. His shoulders will droop. Turning slowly, he will go back to his bedroom, his interest in any further coloring squelched.

Fortunately, that is not the normal response even the busiest mom will give. Instead, she will praise the glories of the picture, say nice things about the colors, and declare it to be some of the best coloring she has ever seen. Then she will say, "Let's put it on the refrigerator so everyone can enjoy it!" Can you see the little kid? His eyes light up! He stands tall! He feels great! His feet are almost unable to touch the floor. He nearly flies back to his bedroom to create an even better work of art. His interest in coloring couldn't be higher. This is motivation at its very best.

Whenever I told the story of the little boy to my class, I would actually draw the rabbit's picture on the board with colored chalk as though I were the little kid. Then I would mimic how the little kid would run up to his mother to show it off. I would approach the desk of one of the girls in class and hold up the imaginary picture. Using my best little kid's voice I would ask, "What is Mommy going to say about my picture?"

Yes, what is Mommy going to say?

One of the banners often used at the front of Redeemer Lutheran Church in Yakima shows two hands, one reaching toward the other. The inscription reads, "Encourage One Another." Those three words say a lot about motivating our fellow Christians. We also can learn a lesson from the story about the little boy.

All too often we ignore the things our children or fellow Christians do. Worse, yet, we criticize their efforts to serve God. The feelings and reactions of adults are not as easily read as those of a little kid. We tend to hide our true feelings, not letting others know when they say something that hurts or discourages us. We all need encouragement just like the imaginary little kid in my classroom illustration. And we have every reason to encourage one another.

Our own efforts to serve God are tarnished because of our sinful nature. Every day we color way outside the lines of God's will. The pictures of our lives are not pretty pictures. Yet God sees them as perfect because of Jesus' blood and righteousness. "The blood of Jesus, his Son, purifies us from all sin" (1 John 1:7). Our lives are beautiful in his sight. "The LORD delights in those who fear him, who put their hope in his unfailing love" (Psalm 147:11). We can encourage others by pointing them to that truth.

We can also encourage others by reminding them that their work done for the Lord is beautiful in his sight. Have you said something positive to a fellow Christian today? Or let a member of the congregation know he or she did something well? Have you complimented the pastor on the work put into the sermons and Bible studies? the organist on the music selections? the choir on its performance? the ladies on the success of the last potluck? Let us make a point of encouraging people who offer their humble works of service to the Lord. Remember, people need their "pictures displayed on the refrigerator."

Hell Roaring Canyon—An Allegory about Faith

One February, Ruth, I, and ten others went to the Big Mountain Resort near Whitefish, Montana, for a ski vacation. I had skied, off and on, for 40 years. Ruth, for 30. Although that is long enough to know something about how to do it, many of the runs are still able to keep us humble.

As we were warming up on one of the longer intermediate runs, I pondered the beauty of the resort. The night before, God had chosen to add a little extra white stuff to trees already heavily laden with snow. In fact, they were so completely covered, it was easy to imagine that something other than live trees formed the center of those unique fluffy shapes. We call them snow ghosts because they all but disappear when low clouds or fog move in.

We launched into the first run of the morning with a certain sense of exhilaration. Our legs were fresh, the run freshly groomed, the air crisp. We glided easily from side to side toward the bottom. The feeling of freedom, the beauty, and the wonder made the effort to get there all worthwhile.

Skiing reminds me of the closeness of God. Perhaps because I can't help but marvel at the power and wisdom that created those majestic, snow-covered mountains. Perhaps because on those mountains, I feel so free of other worldly cares.

Later in the day, we took a lift to the top and dropped down along the edge of Hell Roaring Canyon, a double-diamond slope for experienced skiers only. It's a box canyon. That means once we started down, the only way out was to ski through the canyon for a couple miles until we got to another chairlift.

We went along the canyon edge looking for a good place to start our run. Several hundred yards of open snow beckoned us from the bottom of the steep canyon wall. We were faced with one of those moments when our many years of experience were supposed to come into play. I don't believe we would want to walk down that canyon wall in the summer, and I know we couldn't ride our horses down. But on skis we would have a chance.

Skiing off a bank like that requires a lot of faith in our abilities. If we didn't have the techniques mastered, we would be bound to fall. And if we did fall, we would likely land 60 yards below our skis. To negotiate the turns, we had to do the opposite of what seemed the natural thing to do. We had to lean way out over the edge, plant the down-hill ski pole, put weight on the tip of the lower ski and push off, then repeat the process for each turn. If we leaned back toward the wall, we would fall. In fact, following our logic, which screamed "lean back toward the hill," would have been the perfect recipe for disaster.

The challenge of maneuvering those turns on a steep hillside in Montana is a good object lesson about our Christian faith. Human logic tells us a man who died on a cross two thousand years ago can have little to do with us. Logic tells us it is pointless to entrust our lives to someone we can't see. When bad things happen to Christians, it poses the question of whether God really loves us. Logic tells us we are not good enough and don't deserve to be loved by God. It tells us the treasures of life are the earthly things we can see and touch and buy and sell.

Whenever we come to a crisis in our lives, we want to lean back toward the things we can see rather than forward over the grace of God. We want to stay close to the wall because we aren't sure God's promises are true. We aren't sure they will bring us safely to the end of life's run. But God promises us, "If you make the Most High your dwelling—even the Lord, who is my refuge—then no harm will befall you, no disaster will come near your tent" (Psalm 91:9,10).

Jesus also tells us that if we have faith, we can do hard things: "If you have faith as small as a mustard seed, you can say to this mountain, 'Move from here to there' and it will move. Nothing will be impossible for you" (Matthew 17:20).

We can do hard things, not because our faith is strong but because our faith rests in him who is all powerful. When financial troubles loom before us, we can trust him to provide what we need. When sickness takes us off the trail we had planned to take in life, we can trust that he will make it work out for our good. Glorious and beautiful is the life of a child of God. With our Lord at our side, we can make those turns down the sides of the Hell Roaring Canyons of our lives with confidence.

Learning to trust in the Lord is a lifetime proposition, learned one lesson at a time. Each time we lean back and fail, we turn to God's promises in the Bible to help us up and give us the strength we will need for the next canyon.

Did we get down Hell Roaring Canyon? Yes. Did anyone fall? Yes, we did. But for the most part we navigated the challenging run successfully because, over the years, we had learned to trust our equipment and to trust the lessons we had learned at the school of hard knocks. Do we have more to learn? Yes, there is always another challenge to overcome and another lesson to learn. The same holds true for our faith.

Whether we are longtime veterans of the Christian faith or rank beginners, we need the strength that only the Holy Spirit can give us. We need to continue growing in our faith by regularly studying God's Word. Only then will we be ready when we unexpectedly find ourselves at the top of one of the double-diamond slopes of life.

ONE DAY CLOSER TO HOME

Why are we here on earth? What is our purpose? How long will we be here? Have you ever thought about those questions? Our lives echo with questions—serious questions.

When I was still teaching, I can remember asking myself several questions as I left for home each day. "Why am I doing this? What good am I doing? Will I live long enough to make a difference?" When I got to be 50, I began to think more and more about my own mortality. Now that I am almost 64, I find myself reading the obituaries each day to see if I am listed. That might be a little exaggeration, but not too much. Many of the people I have known over the years are gone now. Granted, many of those were from my folks' generation, but all too many were younger than I am now when they died.

My father lived to be 56. The year I was 56, I often thought about his passing at such an early age. I experienced a certain sense of relief when I turned 57.

While pondering my future the other day, I got out my Bible and found some interesting passages. Romans 8:38,39 tells us, "I am convinced that neither death nor life, neither angels nor demons, neither the present nor the future, nor any powers, neither height nor depth, nor anything else in all creation, will be able to separate us from the love of God that is in Christ Jesus our Lord." That's

God's promise. Nothing can separate us from his love, not now or in the future. In 1 Peter 5:7 we read, "Cast all your anxiety on him because he cares for you." Our all-knowing and all-powerful God cares about us. That should take away a lot of our worries. In the meantime, we have a job to do while we are here on earth—to introduce others to the God who created them and died for them. As recipients of God's love, we can't keep silent about the things God has done for us. Paul tells us, "Christ's love compels us, because we are convinced that…he died for all, that those who live should no longer live for themselves but for him who died for them and was raised again" (2 Corinthians 5:14).

I have come to believe that life is a journey and only God knows what it will bring or how long it will last. But he has revealed to us, his children, where our trip will end. We have a new and better place waiting for us after this life. Each time we watch the sun go down, we are one day closer to home. I find that thought comforting.

One more question. Are you ready if you are called home today?

JUST AT THAT BLINKING OF AN EYELASH

For the men and women who have gone to war, life and death can be measured in split seconds. As horrible as the battles may be, God's children know that God is always there even in the worst of them. Psalm 23 verse 4 voices their confidence: "Even though I walk through the valley of the shadow of death, I will fear no evil, for you are with me."

My uncle Kenneth Mumme was a marine who served his country in the Pacific Theater in WWII and, later, in Korea. Like so many of his generation, he was only 19 years of age when he was sent off to fight in "the valley of the shadow of death." Today Kenneth continues to give the Lord credit for his survival. After reading the following stories, I think you will agree.

In 1942, Kenneth was on a ship that supplied the marines who were fighting for the island of Guadalcanal. A Japanese submarine, primed to fire torpedoes broadside into Kenneth's ship, was spotted and blown up by a passing plane. One night just weeks later, as he stood near gun three on the ship's stern, he spotted two incoming torpedoes. Their wakes were visible against the phosphorus glow of the ocean. Unable to do anything to stop them, he watched until they passed from view—just behind his ship.

On June 15, 1944, the Second Marine Division landed on the island of Saipan. By the second night, Kenneth's unit was positioned on the extreme left flank of the American line. From the foxholes along the beach, the marines in Kenneth's unit watched as American battleships laid down a barrage of artillery shells. They could hear the boom and see each shell streak in a high arc over their positions. But one boom was followed by an eerie momentary silence. Then a short round suddenly exploded just 3 feet from a disabled half-track—perhaps 50 feet from Kenneth's position. Though sand flew everywhere, no one was hurt. Had that shell hit the half-track, the flying shrapnel probably would have killed Kenneth and many others.

That same night, Japanese forces launched a banzai charge against the Americans along the beach road, but the marines stopped them. As the sun rose the next morning, Kenneth was sitting by his foxhole with his dungaree jacket open. Thinking about how tired he was, Kenneth suddenly straightened up, leaned against a sand dune, and tipped his helmet back. Just in that blinking of an eyelash, a sniper's bullet burned its way across his chest like a red hot poker—barely breaking the skin. Kenneth keeled over as if he had been hit and played dead. Another marine killed the sniper.

Three days later, Kenneth was trying to get water from an old well just a hundred yards from Saipan's American headquarters. The area was littered with debris from the wreckage of an old house. Looking for a pan to use to carry the water, he flipped over a large piece of tin roofing. Kenneth jumped when he spotted a Japanese sniper hiding underneath with a large supply of ammo. Recovering quickly, Kenneth grabbed the rifle and wrestled it away from the soldier. If that sniper had been there all day, he easily could have picked off several men without being spotted.

Although the marine forces were battling a variety of diseases, Kenneth lasted until Saipan was nearly secured before coming down with breakbone fever. His fever soared to 105 degrees. Unable to get to a hospital the first night, he survived by lying all night on top of an ammo trailer in a downpour of cool rain.

As a result of the fever, his weight dropped from 175 to 140 pounds and his hair came out in clumps. To this day he is nearly bald.

After securing Saipan, the Second Marine Division attacked and secured the island of Tinian, and then returned to Saipan. In April of 1945, Kenneth's division was sent to the island of Okinawa. One day a chaplain invited any interested marines to join him for a worship service. The small group of marines gathered in a cane field where the chaplain had set up his small portable pulpit. The marines stood in front of the pulpit, while the chaplain put on his white robe and opened his Bible. At the very moment that he looked up to speak, an artillery shell shrieked between the chaplain and the marines and exploded less than 100 yards from the group. Of course, they hit the deck. When they got up, the chaplain dusted the red dirt from his white robe as well as he could. Looking at the marines he said, "Boy, what a way to start a service!"

In one operation Kenneth's rocket squad was told to set up and fire on a certain target. Normally after firing a round of rockets, they would quickly move out because they would have given away their position. However, this time the order came to reload. That meant hand loading 36 rockets while snipers shot at them. One shell came so close its percussion knocked Kenneth's assistant off the launcher. After firing the second round of rockets at the new target, they got out quickly. Later reconnaissance confirmed that they had destroyed a Japanese artillery unit with the first round and an infantry unit with the second. Kenneth came away without a scratch, just a little upset stomach. Just before the firing started, he had taken a bite from a tobacco plug. During the skirmish he swallowed all the tobacco juice because in all the excitement, he had forgotten to spit.

One night Kenneth was on guard duty with a man who always fell asleep. While his companion slept, Kenneth memorized each bush, tree, and rock within his field of vision. Suddenly he noticed something new. A man's silhouette had appeared next to one of the trees. Without waking his partner, Kenneth aimed his M1 Garand semiautomatic rifle and fired several rounds into the darkness. His buddy woke up! The next day they found the man with a bag of grenades he had intended to lob into the American positions.

Kenneth spent the last weeks of the war back on Saipan as the American troops geared up for the expected invasion of the Japanese mainland. His Second Marine Division would have been included in the first wave, which, he discovered later, was expected to incur 100 percent casualties. This, of course, was made unnecessary when the United States dropped the atomic bombs.

Shortly after the war ended, Kenneth returned to civilian life and became active once again in church work. On March 30, 1946, he married my mother's sister, Connie. After their second child was born, Kenneth was called up from the reserves to go to Korea. Because he was a weapon's expert with extensive knowledge about machine guns, bazookas, and rockets, as well as 37-mm, 105-mm, and 155-mm artillery pieces, the military needed his expertise.

Arriving in Korea after the Chinese came into the war, Kenneth took part in what was referred to as leapfrog actions. American troops would fall back on purpose, pulling the enemy into a trap. At one point they put the 155-mm artillery pieces 1,500 yards in front of the lines to harass the Chinese troops. Kenneth and five others were sent beyond the artillery as support. During the daylight hours for five consecutive days, they guarded a single road with bazookas and machine guns in case the Chinese tanks came that way. Each night the squad, along with the artillery units, fell back behind the relative safety of a ridge where the main American line was located. The enemy tanks never arrived while his squad was on point, but word finally came that the Chinese were mounting an attack. Kenneth stayed behind the main lines that day with his artillery unit and their 155-mm guns. As the enemy approached, his unit and three others laid down a deadly wall of exploding steel. The American infantry stopped any Chinese troops they had missed. After the battle was over, they were confronted with the ugly face of war as they surveyed the carpet of bodies that lay before them.

One day, after he picked up his mail, Kenneth walked over to a place where the top military brass had congregated. He wanted to get a better look at the famous general, Douglas MacArthur. When he was only about 75 feet from the general, he idly kicked at what looked like a broom handle sticking out of the ground. His foot came within an inch of the antipersonnel mine before he realized what it was.

Later, when guerrilla fighters began attacking American truck convoys, jeep convoys were sent out as decoys to tempt the enemy into giving away their positions. One day Kenneth's was the lead jeep in a convoy of six that carried American machine-gun squads. As they drove up into a valley, the marines noticed swarms of people high on the surrounding mountainsides. Unwittingly, they had driven right into the enemy's stronghold. Not wanting to let the enemy know they had been spotted, the Americans continued with a routine patrol. The leader of the marine patrol got out of his jeep, talked to local villagers, and returned to the lead jeep. All six jeeps then turned around and left without firing a shot. After they reported what they had seen, however, a marine infantry force was sent into the area and successfully routed the guerrillas.

These stories of hardship and close calls are hard for us to fathom. I often wonder how our generation would fare if faced with similar challenges. We sometimes find it difficult to get to church on Sunday because of a little rain, fog, or ice, or because we have caught a little cold. We don't have to worry about artillery shells disrupting our church services or snipers taking shots at us. Perhaps we should rethink our excuses the next time we are tempted to skip a church service or Bible class.

One of Kenneth's stories stood out from the rest. I could tell by his voice that it had special meaning for him. In a letter his wife, Connie, had sent while he was in Korea, she had included the words of John 14:27: "Peace I leave with you; my peace I give you. I do not give to you as the world gives. Do not let your hearts be troubled and do not be afraid." He read these words again and again: "My peace I give you." One night a marine infantry unit ran by his artillery gun, reporting that the enemy was right behind them. Orders called for the artillery units to explode phosphorus grenades in the artillery pieces to make them unworkable if they were going to be overrun. Kenneth wondered if he had the strength to do what was needed, and then he remembered that verse. At that very moment, he felt someone touch his sleeve and he heard the words "Fear not!" He looked around. No one was there. "But," as he would later tell the story, "the fear was gone." Kenneth had no doubt about what he heard. "Now there is the power of the Lord!" he said with conviction.

That day the enemy was stopped before getting to Kenneth's position.

In 1 Peter 1:6,7, the apostle tells us: "Now for a little while you may have had to suffer grief in all kinds of trials. These have come so that your faith—of greater worth than gold, which perishes even though refined by fire—may be proved genuine and may result in praise, glory and honor when Jesus Christ is revealed." Certainly Kenneth and other veterans were put to the test of fire. He came home to raise a family of four in a Christian environment. He taught Sunday school, sang in the choir, and served continually for the glory of the Lord. Here was a man who easily could have said "Why me, Lord?" or "This is more than I can take!" and given up. But he didn't. His faith in God never faltered. I pray that we might all have such strong faith.

To some, the members of Kenneth's generation are the greatest generation. Perhaps in some ways they were. After their faith and values were shaped and tested by the fire of war, they returned home to make America a nation like none other. We would all do well to look back at the values and strengths of that generation and learn from their example.

One of Kenneth's last comments to me, as I finished interviewing him for this story, was "If you need that strength, call on the Lord!" What a different world it would be if all of us would make that our motto and live it to the fullest!

Truth and Purity

In Revelation 22:17 we read: "The Spirit and the bride say, 'Come!' And let him who hears say, 'Come!' Whoever is thirsty, let him come; and whoever wishes, let him take the free gift of the water of life." The word *bride* is used several times in various places in the Bible to represent the invisible church, the group of all true believers. These are the people who echo the words recorded in Revelation 22:20: "Amen. Come, Lord Jesus." These are people in whose hearts the Holy Spirit lives and works to bring each of us the "free gift of the water of life."

The problem comes when we apply our human logic to the simple fact that we are saved by grace. For some reason that concept is hard for us to accept. Salvation is ours by the grace of God through the sacrifice Christ made on the cross. He took away our sins and made the free gift of salvation possible. Nothing we do earns our salvation. Christ did what had to be done for us. The Holy Spirit was sent to show us that that free gift is ours.

Once the Holy Spirit has entered our hearts bringing the gift of saving faith in Christ, we WANT to do things to please God. We help guide others to a saving faith in Jesus. We worship him publicly and privately. We are kind and generous to others. We work hard at our occupations as if working for the Lord. However, the devil still lurks near us, waiting for an opening to lead us astray. Sometimes he puts temptations in our paths: the desire for material things, love of an unbelieving spouse or friend, troubled family relationships, opportunities to commit adultery, to lie, or to steal. Because the road is so narrow, it isn't easy getting around those obstacles.

Some of the most challenging obstacles for believers are very subtle, like twinges of doubt about God's Word because it doesn't make sense to our human logic. Over time believers may be pulled away from the narrow path of truth until their faith is nothing more than trust in the hollow shell of some misguided philosophy. Truth that has been accepted for generations, in some cases, has been undermined and questioned and eventually discarded. Unfortunately, among the truths tossed in the philosophical wastebasket are such fundamental truths as the creation account, the virgin birth, and Christ's resurrection from the dead, as well as the account of the great flood and what God teaches about homosexuality, marriage, and sex.

But the Holy Spirit is there, whispering in each person's heart and pointing to the truth of God's Word. If we diligently study his Word, the Spirit will guide us with his beacon of truth.

A friend of ours who takes God and studying the Bible seriously attended a Bible class with us. Though she had been raised as a conservative Lutheran, she had spent several years as a member of a liberal church. By God's grace, she returned to her roots. She shared a few passages from a book written by a professor from the church body she had once attended. We were all somewhat taken aback by how far this man's beliefs had strayed from the Bible's truth. One of our friend's comments that evening really hit home for me. After sharing the passage with us, she admitted, "I didn't hold to it (the true teaching of God's Word), but God held on to me!" Upon reflection I see the truth in that statement. Because she knew what the Bible taught and cared enough to keep studying the Word, the Holy Spirit would not let her be comfortable with such liberal teachings. She felt compelled to return to a church that held to the truth.

Study the precious truths of the Bible as if they are the most important treasure you will ever hold. They are. Attend church and Bible studies. Study your Bible and pray on your own. Jesus said in John 8:31,32: "If you hold to my teaching, you are really my disciples. Then you will know the truth, and the truth will set you free." Like a beacon, the Holy Spirit will guide you to the truth. But remember, you can't see a beacon if you turn your back on it.

May God give us all the desire to search for the truth in God's Word, and as that truth is revealed to us, may he give us the strength to hold faithfully to it. Let us pray for others, that God will lead them to know the way that alone leads to life. "Enter through the narrow gate. For wide is the gate and broad is the road that leads to destruction, and many enter through it. But small is the gate and narrow the road that leads to life, and only a few find it" (Matthew 7:13,14).

Mission Work, Our Work!

What does the word *missionary* conjure up in your mind? I get an immediate image of people like Albert Schweitzer, who served as a medical missionary in Africa until his death. Or Dr. Tom Dooley, a Christian who dedicated his medical skills to helping others on the foreign mission field. Or a group of missionaries who were speared to death while trying to reach out to a remote tribe in Ecuador. I think of people I have known personally who served in faraway mission fields such as Thailand or various African countries. I also think of the church of my youth, which sent 50 or 60 people to various Indian reservations in California, Arizona, or Old Mexico each spring break to help with a variety of projects on the mission compounds. I think of a WELS missionary in Bulgaria who reported that the Holy Spirit was attracting so many people to the Sunday services that many people had to stand for the services.

Though it was 20-odd years ago, I still remember a missionary who described how people smuggled Bibles into the old Soviet Union by sewing them into the linings of their overcoats. That might have seemed logical, except it was summer and very hot. The border guards searched all the luggage and the interior of the vehicle thoroughly because they suspected something. However, they never noticed the coats, stiff and heavy because of the Bibles, worn by the sweating mission workers. To be caught with those Bibles would have meant jail time or worse. It would have meant also that people who were hungry for the Word would have had to go without. The guards let them pass.

The life of a missionary is difficult for a number of reasons. Missionaries are usually separated from their extended families for long periods of time—and from their home churches. They forfeit their familiar way of life, the security of good medical care, the food and climate to which they have grown accustomed, and, in some cases, the relative safety of life in the United States. They trust in the Lord and put everything on the line for the work he has commissioned us all to do—spreading the Good News to all the people of the world.

Most of us haven't been called to serve in a foreign mission field. We may not have the gifts to serve that way. However, all of us have the ability to support the missionaries we send in *our* place. The need is great! The need is real! The need is now! Letters, prayers, care packages, and financial support for our church's mission programs are just some of the ways we are able to serve.

To "go and make disciples of all nations" (Matthew 28:19) was not the marching orders of a select few only. That was God's assignment to the entire Christian church. What an awesome privilege God has given us, to bring his good news to the world!

LOST AND FOUND

Do you ever feel that you are going in circles, covering a lot of ground, but getting nowhere? You try to get to church, but something keeps getting in the way. You want to sing in the choir but are afraid to make the necessary commitment. The pastor's new evening Bible study sounds interesting, but when the time comes for the first meeting, you lack the energy. You want to study your Bible at home, but you keep falling asleep. Perhaps you can't seem to find a way out of the thick forest of demands on your time and life. Or maybe you are troubled by something you have done. You feel lost and defeated. Maybe you need a guiding light. We all do.

Several years ago my elk-hunting partner and I had been out all day with little more than sore feet to show for our efforts. Feeling a sense of relief as I neared our camp, I suddenly heard a shot. Then another. And still another. Though it was almost at the end of shooting hours, I was glad someone was having some luck. Since my partner was not back yet, I fed the horses and started to get things set up for the evening meal. As it got later, I began to wonder what had happened to my partner. He normally didn't stay out late in the evening.

I flipped on the CB radio and asked where in the world he was. In the back of my mind, I thought about the shots I had heard earlier. Maybe he had an elk. When no one answered my call, I tried again. Still no answer. Finally, I picked up a voice, though the static drowned all but a few words. The results were no better on the truck CB. Finally, after I walked several yards up the mountain, I was able to determine that he was somewhere south of camp. I thought he said he had an elk down.

I saddled the horses and loaded the equipment we would need to carry an elk back to camp. Then I rode due south for half a mile or so. When I stopped and radioed my partner this time, his message came in much clearer. He had no elk. He was lost! The three shots had been a call for help, but I had completely missed their meaning. I said a little prayer asking God to show me the best way to help my partner find his way out.

When I asked where he thought he was, he replied that he had been at the base of a high ridge, but had gone downhill and wandered around a lot. I knew approximately where he had started, and I also knew that a confusing mixture of thickly forested ridges sprawled all through that area. In the dark, finding the way out could be a real challenge.

He had a small flashlight, but it was going dead. I told him not to move and not to use his light anymore; I had an idea. If it worked, he would be out of that maze in short order. If it didn't, this was going to be one long night for both of us.

South of camp, an abandoned road led to a high knob that was sometimes used as a helicopter pad. From that vantage point, the terrain fell off abruptly in the direction I figured my partner must be.

I tethered the horses on the knob and brought out the large, super-bright flashlight I had intended to use while we dressed the elk. Now I hoped it would help solve a different problem.

This time my partner's voice came back loud and clear over the CB. Because it was very dark, I was able to put my plan into action. I told my partner I was going to switch on my big flashlight and walk slowly around the top of the knob shining the beam down over the whole area. He objected, because he didn't even know where to look. I told him to stay calm and slowly make a 360 degree turn while scanning the horizon for my light. As he did, I walked along the edge of the knob with my light. He couldn't see anything. I made another pass. Still nothing. I then instructed him to move about 30 feet and look for the light as he made another 360 degree turn. Though he was skeptical, he did as I suggested. On about my fourth trip along the edge of the knob, the radio suddenly came to life. "I think I saw it! But I can't see it now!"

I backed up very slowly and waved the light. "I see it!" he shouted.

I then directed him to turn his light on and start toward me. After a while I could see the faintest of lights way down in the canyon below the knob. When his light went dead only a short time later, he was totally dependent on the light from above as he worked his way up the steep hillside to safety and the promise of supper. He was embarrassed but glad to be back where he belonged.

At times we all feel as lost and embarrassed as my partner felt. We seem to travel in circles, unable to find our way in this confusing world. Like my partner, we need a light to show us the way. At those times, we need to get out our Bibles so we can see the brightest light the world has ever known. "I am the light of the world. Whoever follows me will never walk in darkness, but will have the light of life" (John 8:12). We need to get our bearings by finding that light. "The LORD is my light and my salvation—whom shall I fear? The LORD is the stronghold of my life—of whom shall I be afraid?" (Psalm 27:1). If our own light of faith is flickering, we have his comforting promise: "A bruised reed he will not break, and a smoldering wick he will not snuff out" (Isaiah 42:3). And if we have wandered away from God's light, we remember the words of Jesus that there is great joy in heaven when a lost sinner is found.

In his parable of the prodigal son, Jesus told of a father who joyfully welcomed his lost son back with no reservations. "We had to celebrate and be glad, because this brother of yours was dead and is alive again; he was lost and is found" (Luke 15:32).

God answered my prayer that night with a light and provided a way to bring my lost partner back into our elk camp. Infinitely more important is the light that guides lost souls back into God's camp. May God keep our eyes focused on the light of the world.

ON AGING AND DEATH

A few years ago when a friend died, I began thinking about aging, death, and the questions and fears people have about the whole process. My reflections inspired me to write the following poem about the passage of time. I share it here for the first time.

Our Sands of Time on Earth

They pass swiftly through the storm-darkened nights.
Bits of sand shining in the fading glow of light.
Thoughts about their end, a kaleidoscope of frights.
Our eyes peer; questioning the numbers gone in flight.
But their passage dims our perceptions and sight.
They pass swiftly through the storm-darkened nights.
How many more are left waiting for the coming fall?
Does anyone really know when the Master will call?
Thoughts about their end, a kaleidoscope of frights.
We struggle desperately to hold them back at all cost,
But we're judged powerless and to us they're lost.
They pass swiftly through the storm-darkened nights.
Their numbers are counted and carefully hidden by us.
Though their yearly passage causes others to fuss.
Thoughts about their end, a kaleidoscope of frights.
Exercise and cosmetics argue against their passage.
Questions, thoughts, wonders; sands seek the final page.

They pass swiftly through the storm-darkened nights.
Thoughts about their end, a kaleidoscope of frights.

Time passes much more swiftly for adults than for kids. We hardly start a new year before we are celebrating Christmas and New Year again. As time passes, our bodies change. The aches, pains, and illnesses of youth didn't last long. As we get older, the aches accumulate, the pains linger, and the illnesses slow us down. No matter how hard we try to stay young, no matter how hard we work at trying to stop this aging process, no matter how many billions of dollars our society spends on medicines, cosmetics, hair transplants, and facelifts—trying to hide the ravages of time—our bodies change with age. And as our bodies age, we tend to spend more and more time thinking about our own mortality. We tend to view age differently.

Perhaps our thinking begins to change the first time we say to a younger person: "That's right. You are too young to remember way back in the eighties." Or when the music and movies we grew up with are referred to as "classics." Yes, the more time passes, the more we become aware of our mortality. How blessed we Christians are that, unlike the rest of society, we have hope through the sacrifice Christ made for us.

Our relatively short time on this earth is a time of God's grace. From the time we're born, God works to make us aware of the great sacrifice Christ offered for us. Where would we be without the knowledge that God loved us enough to send his Son to save us from our sins and to defeat, once and for all, the sting of death. Knowing this protects us from needless worries about aging, illness, and death. They are all part of life.

Our lives on earth are but a flash of light when compared to the time we will spend in heaven. Our brief journey here is the time God uses to prepare us for that eternity. The aging process is not something we need to dread or despise. God uses it to get us to relax our hold on this earth and to turn our eyes toward heaven.

A line in a "classic" song from long ago said something to the effect that everybody wants to go to heaven, but nobody wants to die. I have always found those words interesting. As Christians we need not fear death. In fact, when our time on earth is up, we can welcome death because we know the best is yet to come.

"'Where, O death, is your victory? Where, O death, is your sting?' The sting of death is sin, and the power of sin is the law. But thanks be to God! He gives us the victory through our Lord Jesus Christ.

"Therefore, my dear brothers, stand firm. Let nothing move you. Always give yourselves fully to the work of the Lord, because you know that your labor in the Lord is not in vain" (1 Corinthians 15:55-58).

I'VE GOT THE REST OF MY LIFE!

You know, one of these days I will get around to setting things straight with the Lord. One of these days I'll be more regular about going to church. One of these days I'll attend those Bible classes. One of these days I'll get my kids to Sunday school and I'll tell them why it's important. One of these days I'll join the choir. One of these days we'll start a family prayer time. One of these days I'll help with a church project. One of these days I'll start attending church meetings. One of these days I'll tell a friend why the Lord is important to me. But I've got the rest of my life!

On April 15, 1999, my wife's brother was having his morning coffee before leaving for work. It was an ordinary day. There was no reason to expect anything unusual. His wife and several of his children were in the house with him. Suddenly, with no warning, he slumped over. He was gone before he hit the floor. At 49 years of age, he had suffered a massive heart attack.

Have you stopped to consider that this could be your last day? Our lives are sometimes a lot shorter than we plan!

At her brother's funeral, Ruth sang a well-known hymn, "On Eagles' Wings." Based on Isaiah 40:31, the words of the hymn confess our confidence that the Lord will give strength and help to those who trust in him. "Those who hope in the LORD will renew their strength. They will soar on wings like eagles; they will run and not grow weary, they will walk and not be faint."

God has a purpose and a plan for each of us. Sometimes as we carry out his plan, we run into obstacles and experience hardships that discourage us. His promise of eternal life through Christ gives the purpose in our lives and offers hope and strength to overcome the obstacles and endure the hardships as we carry out God's purpose. The uncertainty about the length of our lives urges us to do the things that are important today. We can't afford to let another day go by without taking the reins of spiritual leadership for our families or using our gifts for the good of our church and the kingdom of God on earth. There may not be another day.

MAKE YOUR HOUSE YOUR HOME

It takes a lot of living to make a house a home. It may take even more effort to physically keep it in good shape. If the roof leaks, we quickly fix it. A broken pipe results in a call to a plumber. When a lightbulb burns out, we replace it. We call the cleaners whenever the rugs look a little soiled. Every few years, we paint the house inside and out, to give it a fresh clean look. We do all of this in addition to the daily housecleaning.

And the longer we live in them, the more our homes become an extension of ourselves. We make our houses *our homes* by decorating and furnishing them *our way.* We invest in all sorts of trappings to make them just the way we want them. It is fair to say we put our very hearts and souls into our homes. We expend a lot of blood, sweat, and tears to accomplish the finished products. We do our best to protect them from robbery, fire, or other catastrophes. We worry whether we have enough insurance. But insurance, we realize, can only replace the building and other *things.* Insurance can't replace the keepsakes and memories that went into making our homes.

Likewise, it takes a heap of living and lots of work on God's part to mold our Christian faith into what it needs to be. I am not talking about doing good works and earning our way into heaven. Our salvation comes by grace. It is a gift. I am speaking instead about our lives after we receive that gift.

Satan is busy trying to take advantage of weaknesses in the structure of our faith in order to knock it down. He tries to poke holes in the roof so the philosophies of the world will seep in and rot the very core of our faith. He tries to soil our lives by smearing the outer walls with hatred and unkindness. He spatters the inside with greed and lust. He short-circuits our thinking, so we begin to enjoy those things, and hopes we eventually abandon our faith entirely. Jesus recognizes the destruction caused by Satan and his crew. Jesus knows that if we give Satan a chance to work in our homes, all may be lost.

When Satan attacked Jesus with his wilderness temptations, Jesus knew that the key to survival was found in the Word of God. That is the key to our survival also.

Many people make the mistake of thinking that once they are baptized and confirmed, their spiritual houses are in order and need no further care. If we think that way, Jesus' warning through Paul gives us reason to think again. "So, if you think you are standing firm, be careful that you don't fall!" (1 Corinthians 10:12). The foundation of our faith is laid by the Holy Spirit working through Baptism and God's Word. The Spirit continues to build and repair and rebuild through the preaching of the good news of Jesus and through the Lord's Supper. "Faith comes from hearing the message, and the message is heard through the word of Christ," the apostle Paul wrote in Romans 10:17. Whenever we hear or read the words of Scripture, the Spirit works to strengthen our faith. Let us give ourselves all the chances we can to hear him by regularly attending church and joining Bible studies whenever possible. As we continue to nurture our Christian faith, it, like our homes, will be beautiful in the sight of God and a blessing to his kingdom.

———— • ————

BIBLE STUDIES
MAKE A DIFFERENCE
IN MORE WAYS THAN ONE

Several years ago Leroy and Phyllis Miller opened their home as a meeting place for a series of Bible studies. At the time, Ruth and I hadn't attended many evening Bible studies, so this was something of a new experience.

One of the blessings we took away from those meetings was the sense of fellowship and camaraderie that developed. We always began each session with an activity that helped us get to know one another a little better. For example, one time we went around the circle telling something about the community where we grew up. Another time we talked about our favorite hobbies. Each week we shared a part of ourselves with our fellow Christians and, of course, they shared with us. We had a lot of fun. We joked, laughed, and sometimes cried over our shared experiences. And as the weeks passed, the members of the group came closer together. We learned a lot about one another: interests, personalities, jobs, and opinions. In those few weeks we got to know one another better than we would have through ten years of formal Sunday morning church services. For Ruth and me, this was a really big step toward becoming a more integral part of our church family.

I believe Bible studies are very important for a variety of reasons. First and foremost is the fact that through the careful, thoughtful study of God's Word, we grow in the knowledge of God's grace, and the Holy Spirit nurtures our faith. An advantage of studying the Bible together with a group of fellow Christians is that as we grow in faith, we also get to know our fellow Christians better. After taking part in this series of Bible studies, Sunday mornings seemed like a time with family. And when it came time to serve the Lord by working on other projects at church, we felt much more comfortable working with people we had come to know. By getting to know one another better, we were also able to pray more specifically for the members of our Christian family when they needed our prayers and to encourage them more regularly when they needed encouragement. Our Lord had those things in mind when he inspired the holy writer to pen these words: "Let us not give up meeting together, as some are in the habit of doing, but let us encourage one another—and all the more as you see the Day approaching" (Hebrews 10:25).

SPECIAL REASON TO BE THANKFUL

Do you have special memories of places or events that show the wondrous things God has put on this earth for us to enjoy? Most everyone does. Without much trouble, we can probably think of a time or a place where the wonders of God seemed to jump out at us. I like to dig through my collection of special memories when I am down and maybe not as thankful as I should be. I would like to share one such special memory.

The stars shown brightly at 4:30 A.M. when I stepped out of my camper at the end of the road. The air was brisk: the mercury had dropped to the 25-degree mark. Knowing that I was about to feed them, the horses whinnied softly. As my hunting partner and I ate a light breakfast, we reflected on the blanket of fresh snow laid down by a late night storm. The heavenly crystals were a welcome change from the rain that had drenched the area for several days. Wet hunting clothes clinging to clammy skin can discourage even the most avid hunter. But on this day, the conditions were perfect. Perfect temperature and perfect snow cover for tracking elk.

Our strategy was simple: get an early start, ride the horses up the mountain—high above the hunters who walked—tether the horses, and hunt there for the morning.

The leather creaked as we saddled our horses and packed the rifles and necessary gear in the dim light of a gas lantern. We had hopes of a great hunt with a chance at one of those elusive bull elk. As it turned out we received much more.

Though it was so dark under the trees that we literally couldn't see our hands in front of our faces, we had been up the mountain on this particular trail often enough that the horses knew exactly where to go. Much of our success—and safety—depended on our surefooted companions. Periodically we emerged from under the canopy of trees to be greeted by a myriad of stars in the clear night sky. Somewhere in the dark a hoot owl gave his mournful call.

Around two thirds of the way up, the trail broke out of the trees and continued parallel to the edge of a cliff, about 20 feet in. The headlights of hunters' cars zigzagged up the distant hills as the red fingers of dawn began to climb over the eastern horizon. Before long, we could see enough to make out shapes.

Nothing can match the experience: searching for sounds in the quiet night, riding on fresh snow far away from other people, listening as the saddles creaked and the horses puffed, and watching a beautiful sunrise as the stars faded into morning.

Near the top, horses and riders passed between two brushy trees onto the edge of an 800-foot cliff. In the semi-darkness we could scan miles of forested country, the distant outline of some pine-topped hills, and beyond them, majestic Mount Rainier. For the next 200 feet, the narrow trail was really dicey. We leaned toward the side of the mountain and rode with only the tips of our boots in the stirrups. Then we were able to cut back into the trees where we tied the horses for the morning hunt.

Yes, we were successful that day. We did bring home meat. But that's not what I remember most. Etched in my memory are the sights and sounds of the magnificent morning: the wonderful ride through the trees and along the cliffs, the stars shining brightly in the moonless sky, the owl's mournful call from deep within the darkness, the swish of the horses' hooves through the fresh snow, and the sunrise breaking over the cloudy horizon. I am truly thankful that God made it possible for my partner and me to experience that morning with all its wonder and beauty.

In this day and age with all the terrible things we see happening in our world, it helps to stop and remember that God gave us many beautiful and good things to enjoy. We have every reason to rejoice with the psalmist who said, "This is the day the LORD has made; let us rejoice and be glad in it" (Psalm 118:24). Think about your special times and places. Each time you do, take a moment to thank the One who makes them possible.

SCHOOL'S IN!

When I was teaching school, I could recognize patterns in the performance of the various students in my classes. Those who were there from the first day did better. It took a very bright student to come in a week late and do well. Students who were there each day did better than those who missed days. The more days they missed, the worse their performance. There was a huge difference in the level of achievement between those lucky students whose parents took a genuine interest in their work at school compared with those whose parents were too busy. That one factor seemed more significant than any other.

Over the years I also consistently observed that the number of parents who came to visit any given class for the open house corresponded very closely to the level of achievement of students in that class. I could predict ahead of time that few, if any, parents of the students in the slow learner programs would come. It was sad, because those were the parents I needed and wanted to see the most.

Have you thought about how the dynamics in a Sunday school class work much the same as those in a public school class? I believe Christian parents want their children raised in the Word. They want them to know the Bible stories and to know Jesus, the Savior of the world. They want them to come to church on their own and to become contributing members of their church family. But these things won't happen unless we take the reins of leadership and show our children how important this is to us and to them. If we pray with them and read the Bible to them, if we talk to them about spiritual things, if we are in Bible class ourselves, if we bring them to Sunday school right from the start—and bring them consistently—if we talk to them about the lessons they learned and take an interest in their projects, they will see how important these things are. It will make a real difference, both on how much our children will learn and how much they will enjoy what they are doing. Thirty years in public education, observing students whose parents took the time to work with them, convinces me that this is so. I have seen the glow of their success. I know that your children will grow too as you take an active role in their spiritual education.

Jesus said, "Let the little children come to me, and do not hinder them, for the kingdom of heaven belongs to such as these" (Matthew 19:14). Those are important words for every parent to take to heart.

THE DEBT IS PAID IN FULL

As my father was slowly dying of multiple myeloma back in the early 1970s, quite a few bills began to accumulate. His brothers—partners in the ranch he had managed for years—continued to pay his salary, and Dad continued to do as much of the paperwork as he could to help run the ranch. It made him feel worthwhile and took his mind off the terrible disease ravaging his body; but the salary couldn't cover his growing debts.

My father was a tough, stubborn man who had not wanted to admit that he was ill. Before the disease was diagnosed, he devised ways of pulling the sprinkler hoses without bending over. The pain in his back was just too intense. He figured out creative ways to save his energy and to avoid the pain that continued to worsen each day. He even went ahead with his scheduled carpal tunnel surgery to cure the numbness in his hands. The doctors never suspected that something far more sinister was at work in his body.

Dad had worked hard all his life and took pride in the fact that he paid his debts. He did not like to owe anyone. However, over time as he became more and more ill, the bills grew larger and larger. There just wasn't enough money to go around.

My maternal grandfather quietly stepped forward and loaned my folks several thousand dollars. At Dad's insistence they wrote a legal contract stating the amount that they owed.

Not long after the contract was signed, my father was called to be with his Lord. A couple of days after the funeral, I came across the contract as I was helping my mother get her papers and finances in order. Later the same day when my grandfather came for a visit, I took him aside. I explained that in order to help my mother set up a plan for taking care of her finances, he should tell us how he would like us to pay the loan. He looked at me, and I can remember his words as if he were saying them now. "Let me see that contract." Then, without any hesitation, he tore it into pieces and deposited it in the garbage can. The debt Dad had owed was paid in full through the Christian goodwill of my grandfather. The slate was clean, not because my father paid it but because it was forgiven. The payment was not for work done, it was a freely given gift from a father who loved his daughter and son-in-law.

Think about what our heavenly Father has done for us, not because we earned it but because he loved us. We are all burdened by huge debts composed of a lifetime of sins. No matter how hard or how stubbornly we work, we cannot pay them. No matter how much we might want to, we cannot follow the directives of the contract laid out in the Ten Commandments. However, through Christ's sacrifice on the cross, we have been redeemed. Our debts have been forgiven, and the slate has been wiped clean. When we die, God will look at us as if we had never sinned, because Christ has paid the full price for our salvation. "In him we have redemption through his blood, the forgiveness of sins, in accordance with the riches of God's grace that he lavished on us with all wisdom and understanding" (Ephesians 1:7,8).

Working for Your Lord Can Make Your Day

One Sunday our pastor announced that we would have a work day to spruce up the church and grounds for the coming Holy Week and Easter celebrations. Since I was serving as president of our small congregation, I got up after the pastor and announced that the work would begin at 9:03 A.M. on Saturday. I explained that I was setting an odd time so they would remember to come. That got a smile.

However, I wasn't smiling when I got up Saturday morning. Nothing seemed to go right. I was grouchy when my wife spoke to me. When I got to my coffee group late and discovered that they had all left to go skiing for the day, I thought to myself, *I can see how this day is going to go.*

I said a little prayer as I drove over to the church. The pastor and I talked briefly as we waited for people to arrive. We didn't have a big plan. We just needed to get things cleaned up.

It is wonderful to see how the Lord works. As it turned out, we needed a pickup to haul red rock for the flower beds. One was there. We needed shrubs trimmed. Two electric trimmers arrived. Rakes were needed. We had five or six. We needed a lightweight ladder to help us reach the windows. Someone had brought one. We needed to haul the trash. Another pickup arrived. We needed loppers. Two sets appeared. We needed to haul the big trimmings. Still another pickup. And with a lot of stomping, and a little rope to tie it down, another whole load was squeezed on that same truck. When I cut some additional dead stuff out of the evergreen trees, it seemed that we had nowhere to put it. One of the guys suggested putting it in the green Dumpster that was already over half full. To the wonder of those who watched, we cut and stomped and fit it all in. Windows were washed. Floors were cleaned and waxed. Every time something needed to be done, someone was available to do it.

By the time our work day for the Lord was over, 25 or so people had pitched in to help. We worked together, enjoyed a neat time of fellowship, and were done in about two and a half hours. We had worked hard, but we felt good when we were through because God's house looked better than ever.

What about my grouchy day? It vanished sometime after I arrived at church and saw the wonder of 25 people working hard for their Lord. It's difficult to stay grouchy when one is touched by the effects of Christian fellowship. Enthusiastic Christian efforts are very contagious: we all caught a case of them that day. "Christ's love compels us, because we are convinced...he died for all, that those who live should no longer live for themselves but for him who died for them and was raised again" (2 Corinthians 5:14,15).

A NOTE ABOUT MARRIAGE

Ruth and I were married on June 14, 1975. During the years since then, we have seen lots of things happen. It's important that our marriage was built on a sturdy foundation.

One thing we agreed upon at the beginning of our relationship was that we would make the church and the Lord's work an integral part of our married life. Ruth and I were married at Redeemer, and I was confirmed there. My son's memorial service was there. In 1977 I went to my first voter's meeting and was elected secretary of the church council at that meeting. Ruth, of course, was involved in activities at the church long before we were married. Over the years, she had taught Sunday school, worked on special programs, directed the choir, been active in the women's group, and held offices in the Lutheran Women's Missionary Society. I haven't actually counted, but I believe I have held one church office or another for well over half the time we have been married. And since we both retired in 1994, we have had even more time for the Lord's work.

I would be the first to admit that our marriage isn't perfect. We have had our disagreements and temptations. The stress of running a tight schedule with both of us teaching, going to meetings, making trips, going to night school, helping relatives, meeting church obligations, and attending social functions has caused a certain amount of friction. We have also had our share of illnesses and deaths in our family and extended family. The key to our enduring marriage has not only been our love for each other, but also our shared partnership with our Lord and our church. With the Lord's help we have supported each other along the way through good times and bad.

Ruth and I are not perfect examples of what a Christian should be either. The only perfect example is Christ. We both readily admit we have made mistakes and that we will no doubt continue to make them. We have strayed from the path more than once. However, as a team, we have struggled through the rough times, and as a team, we have enjoyed the happy times. I believe we have grown closer over the years as we have come to understand each other better and as we have become more involved in our church work. Our faith in God has been the one firm hand we could hold on to in our marriage. There has never been any question about its importance.

Several years ago I wrote a poem for Ruth. I take the liberty of including it here to help celebrate many years with a wonderful partner.

Special Thoughts for My Wife

Warm, close feelings are always there.
Shy eyes meet softly; deeply embraced.
Sometimes distance seems too much to bear.
Talk is tentative; gentle words are shared.
One to the other, our secret souls are bared.
Warm, close feelings are always there.
Welcome smiles give hope to my weary mind;
She lacks the nature to be unkind.
Sometimes distance seems too much to bear.
Images of her come to mind, one then another:

Elegant, beautiful, understanding, softly tender.
Warm, close feelings are always there.
Hair gleaming as if laced with moonlight,
Shape and form an artist's would-be delight.
Sometimes distance seems too much to bear.
Strong willed, irritating, frustrating,
Yet vulnerable, loving, and ever caring.
Warm, close feelings are always there.
Soft as petals of blossoming spring flowers
Shining beautifully in sun-filled April showers.
Warm, close feelings are always there.
Sometimes distance seems too much to bear.

I have truly been blessed during the years of our marriage. I am not easy to live with. Yet, through it all, I've had my partner by my side. Thanks, Ruth, and thank you, Jesus, for being there for us through the years.

June is the month many couples choose for their weddings. Whenever the wedding takes place, I hope every couple will be blessed as we were to find partners to share their lives. I pray they will include the Lord as a third partner. It makes all the difference!

THE LITTLE CHURCH THAT CAN

When the members of a church decide to work together and use all their talents, they can't lose, even when they don't win. It really doesn't matter whether the members are playing in a church softball tournament or working for the Lord.

The Sunday before our church's annual softball tournament, I got up after the service and showed the congregation the huge softball trophy that bore the name of one of our members. It was a trophy Redeemer Lutheran Church had never won. "It would certainly be nice if we could keep this trophy for the whole year since the tournament was named in honor of one of our members," I told the congregation. Many of the church members were relatively new and didn't even know about the trophy. But seeing it and hearing about it generated some interest in the upcoming games. That afternoon we were able to put together a team for our one and only practice. Though some of us hadn't played softball in 30 years, we gave it a go.

The day of the tournament dawned bright and sunny. Though some of us weren't all that talented, we had a good turnout of players—and our spirit was endless. One family had bought T-shirts sporting the church insignia for the team. This helped us feel unified. Quite a few people came to cheer for us throughout the day. That helped too.

We played confidently for our first game, but lost. That meant we had to win seven games in a row to win the trophy. Playing a little harder and with a bit more fire, we won the next three games. But when we fell behind in the fifth game, we got frustrated and began to lose confidence. Then it happened! While Gail, our pitcher and coach, was watching for a ball to be tossed in from the sidelines, the umpire fired a new ball from home plate and hit Gail in the face. The impact knocked him down, broke his glasses, and left a nasty cut under his eye. For a few seconds nobody moved. Then we all ran out to the mound to see if he was okay. Blood was running down his face, and he had been all but knocked out. After we got him over to the sidelines and iced his injury, we could clearly see that he needed stitches.

After Gail's wife took him to the hospital, we resumed the game. An unspoken goal to "win one for the Gipper" began to show itself. We played harder than ever. We hit the ball and made plays that we hadn't seen in the first part of the game. Although it was a tough, close game, we came out on top.

It was an hour before the start of our next game. We were just taking our place on the field when Gail came walking back over to the bench. He didn't play again, but he coached, even though he had to keep an ice pack on the stitches. Again we made the plays and hit the ball, and again we prevailed. The same for the next game. Then we were just one game away from having that trophy, a goal no one had seriously considered.

The team we played for the championship was from a church on the west side of the Cascades, a church four times the size of ours. Having played several more games than our opponent, our team was tired. And though we gave it our all, we ultimately lost.

The opposing team deserved to win. They not only had talent, but they had played and practiced often before the tournament. However, the score was very close! There wasn't a blowout that day!

After the church service that Sunday, I had the whole team and all the helpers come to the front of the church. As they came up the aisle our organist played the theme from *Rocky*. It was great! We were satisfied with our performance. We had played hard, used all our talents, and we were the champions on the east side of the Cascades. As it turned out, a couple of weeks later we were awarded the sportsmanship trophy. So we had a trophy to display after all.

As Christians, we are part of a team dedicated to winning for our Lord. And we will be winners if we apply our talents with the confidence that the Lord will use our particular church and its work to fulfill his will. We may not literally win all the games as we would like. But always keep in mind, the Lord has a purpose for everything. God promises us that our faithful service will never be in vain. May God move all of us to use our talents to further his work. The prize for our efforts is greater than any fancy trophy; it is the commendation from the Lord: "Well done, good and faithful servant!" (Matthew 25:23).

KEEP FOCUSED ON CHRIST

In our rush-here-and-there world, we so easily lose our sense of direction and purpose. As we navigate the challenging and frustrating passages of life, we need to pray for God's guidance. And we need to listen carefully to Jesus as he speaks to us in his Word.

Some of us have ongoing health problems. Others have fears that must be conquered. Sleep won't come. The list of things to do keeps on growing. Our goals become clouded. We even begin to question if our goals are still important or correct. Sometimes we get so tied up and frustrated that we forget where to turn for help. I have had some of those nights. One night years ago, I sat up and wrote this poem to try to express how frustrated and lost I felt.

Night Spirits

The night spirits haunt my soul.
Hopes become shadows; can I really win?
At every bend phantoms shroud my goal.
Turn, turn, then turn still again.
Only to find where once I've been.
The night spirits haunt my soul.
Frustration reigns morning, noon, and night.
At every bend the phantoms shroud my goal.
Great needs on this side, great wants on that.

Run here, run there, run faster! My turn at bat?
The night spirits haunt my soul.
Red jungles of tape entwine my mind.
Looking without seeing. Are they blind?
At every bend phantoms shroud my goal.
Words, sounds, and words are said.
Can't they come to rest in someone's head?
The night spirits haunt my soul.
At every bend phantoms shroud my goal.

God answers our prayers. In his Word, he addresses our frustrations. His plan may not always take the same path ours does, but his plan is a good one. "'I know the plans I have for you,' declares the LORD, 'plans to prosper you and not to harm you, plans to give you hope and a future'" (Jeremiah 29:11). And his plan is good, even if it includes suffering. "We also rejoice in our sufferings, because we know that suffering produces perseverance; perseverance, character; and character, hope. And hope does not disappoint us, because God has poured out his love into our hearts by the Holy Spirit, whom he has given us" (Romans 5:3-5).

The psalmist gives us further comfort: "My flesh and my heart may fail, but God is the strength of my heart and my portion forever" (Psalm 73:26).

When suffering comes our way, we can ask God to remove it or to help us see how he blesses us through it. When we grow weak, we can rest our hearts on the promises of Christ, who encouraged his disciples: "The Counselor, the Holy Spirit, whom the Father will send in my name, will teach you all things and will remind you of everything I have said to you. Peace I leave with you; my peace I give you. I do not give to you as the world gives. Do not let your hearts be troubled and do not be afraid" (John 14:26,27). Let us pray each day that the Counselor we were promised will continue to light the paths we take, especially when our paths seem blocked and the obstacles appear overwhelming.

———— ∗ ————

FEED MY QUAIL—A PARABLE

When the first snow of the season hid the food that sustained the wild birds, my wife and I decided we would feed them. We already had regular bird feeders hanging in the trees, but we were concerned about the many quail that lived in the area. Taking the top off an old coffee table, we set it up between two logs to form a covered feeding area. We purchased finely ground corn, called scratch, and spread it out under the covered feeder. We also scattered some all around so that the shy quail would find their way to the life-giving food.

We waited and watched. The first day only a couple quail found the place that would be their salvation through the dark winter months. The second day, five or six quail pecked nervously at the feed. They didn't want to leave the only source of sustenance in the area. Whether they had simply followed the original quail, or whether our first guests had somehow been able to communicate to the others about the source of food, we do not know. As the weeks wore on, however, more and more quail visited our feeder. They became more bold, flying away only if we came outside or if something else scared them—but they never went very far. After waiting a bit, one would venture back to feed. Soon others would follow.

Before long, we had a covey of more than 40 birds. It was neat to see how they looked out for one another. If one became worried and ran, that signaled the rest to run. If they were eating, they all seemed content.

As the numbers continued to grow throughout the winter, we enlarged the feeder and offered food more often. Soon several coveys visited regularly at various times of the day. They all had one thing in common, a hunger for the life-sustaining food they always found at the feeder. Once they had found the feeder, they were content, and they tried their best to stay close by. They came to realize that the feeder meant a good, healthy, secure life. Life was much harder when they wandered from the feeder.

There are several messages in this story for us as Christians. Can you see them?

"Jesus declared, 'I am the bread of life. He who comes to me will never go hungry, and he who believes in me will never be thirsty'" (John 6:35).

CHURCH?

Look up the word *church* in a dictionary, and you will find definitions that speak of a place, an institution or, perhaps, a reference to an activity. When I think of *church,* I think of our Christian family, all the people around the world who follow Christ. Paul spoke of the church in terms of a personal relationship among fellow Christians and often compared it to the human body. "The body is a unit, though it is made up of many parts; and though all its parts are many, they form one body. So it is with Christ. For we were all baptized by one Spirit into one body—whether Jews or Greeks, slave or free—and we were all given the one Spirit to drink" (1 Corinthians 12:12,13).

In order for our body (church) to work well, all parts must work together for the good of the whole. If one part works against the others or one part is sick, the body doesn't function well. And if one part is missing, the body falters.

Each part is necessary, though not in the same way. Some parts are readily seen by all. Other parts, though just as important, are hidden from view. Each part carries out a vital, necessary task for the body to function properly.

Each of us is a part of the church "body," and each of us carries out an important role. The next time you attend church, look around. But look past the building. Look at each person. What does each person need? What does each person contribute to the church "body"? Ask yourself the questions: "Where do I fit in? Am I faithfully carrying out my role?"

It is vitally important to hear the Word of God at the service on Sunday morning. It is great to put money in the collection plate and shake hands with the pastor on your way out. However, being a part of the church "body" means being involved with the other members of the body in service to God. We can't walk out of the kind of church I'm talking about. We are a part of this church body every minute of every day, all week long.

The free gift of salvation Jesus has won for us inspires us to ask what we can contribute to the body. Here are a few suggestions:

1. We can use our God-given talents to serve God and his people.

2. We can set aside every Sunday as an opportunity to encourage our fellow believers by worshiping together with them.

3. We can make sure we don't simply watch but actually participate in each service.

4. We can consciously apply the sermon to our lives.

5. We can discuss the sermon with someone who was in church, and we can explain the message to someone who wasn't.

6. We can volunteer when we see a need.

7. We can show our thanks to God and serve others through our regular offerings.

8. We can offer encouraging words to those, including the pastor, who serve well. (One of my favorite ways to encourage our

pastor is to sit close to the front during worship services and Bible studies. Watch the effect on the pastor and note how much more you may learn. Try it. You may never sit in the back again.)

9. We can anonymously help someone, for no particular reason.

10. We can fight the temptation to criticize others.

This gives a whole new meaning to our customary greeting "See you in church," doesn't it?

Keeping Our Batteries Charged for the Lord!

Do you ever wake up feeling as though you never went to bed? I can remember feeling that way when I was still teaching. I often arose at 5:00 A.M. to go over the day's lesson for the Advanced Placement class. This helped me feel at least somewhat adequate while teaching American history to 20 or 30 of the smartest history students in the junior class.

Rising at 5:00 A.M. wouldn't have been so bad except that Ruth and I had things going on almost every evening. We often stayed up later than we really should have, only to get up at 5:00 A.M. and start all over again. As a sort of a joke, we developed a regular morning routine. We would look in the mirror and say, "Plop, plop, fizz, fizz. It's show time!" That was a line from the movie *All That Jazz*. In the movie, the responsibility of putting on a Broadway show forced the main character to live on pills, hardly sleeping at all. Every morning he looked at his red eyes in the mirror, took a handful of pills, and said something like "Plop, plop, fizz, fizz. It's show time!" But the grueling schedule gradually wore down his health until he died of a heart attack.

After our little morning routine, I would get out my materials, turn on the Tijuana Brass music, and start working.

In some ways, teaching school is a lot like putting on a show. Not only does the teacher need to know the lines— the materials—but he or she is constantly trying to find ways to keep the students interested and, yes, entertained.

Now that we are out of the school rat race and have had time to reflect, we realize that that schedule didn't do our health any good. I have a feeling a lot of people get themselves into similar rat races.

When our to-do lists drive our lives, we just can't seem to give ourselves permission to take time to recharge our batteries. But that is exactly what we need to do. A time to rest is necessary for both our physical and spiritual health.

God set an example for us by setting aside the seventh day as a day of rest. As we rest our bodies, we also find rest for our souls in listening to the preaching of the Word. In God's promise of eternal life in Christ, we find that which releases us from the misplaced priorities that often consume our lives and wear us down.

God wants us to do his work faithfully. He also wants us to recharge our batteries as we gather with our fellow Christians to refresh our souls at the banquet he offers us each day of worship. Remember the words of Isaiah 40:31: "Those who hope in the LORD will renew their strength."

Dealing with Worry

One day I volunteered to help a cattle rancher gather his cows from the fall range to return them to the lower pastures for the winter. This process usually takes about 30-plus days. At that time he had cattle pastured over an area of about 45,000 acres—some Forest Service land and some privately owned land. The whole region was a mixture of open areas and densely packed forest groves.

On this particular day, we were to ride from where Jump Off Road plateaued up to the power lines at the top. Since, as the crow flies, that was only about five miles, the assignment didn't sound too bad. Five miles up and five miles back. The catch was that we were supposed to zigzag back and forth to find all the cattle in a mile-wide area, to start them down the trails as we went. By the time we were finished, the five-mile ride to the top turned into eight or nine miles. And the ride back was not a whole lot shorter. We had to comb the hillside, working from the left to the far right and back, again and again and again, trying our best not to miss any cows in the thick trees or in the small canyons. By day's end we were pretty worn out.

That long ride moving those cattle reminded me of the way we deal with worry. We see a possible problem on the left and five more on the right and turn our problems into a long, long ride. Pretty soon we see problems everywhere we look.

The things we worry about seldom actually happen, but we expend so much energy playing out all the different scenarios that we fail to resolve our real problems. Worry just keeps delaying the solution. It's like spinning the wheels on your car. It uses a lot of energy, makes a lot of noise, and wears off a lot of the tires, but nothing of value happens.

If we could have known exactly where the cows were, we could have ridden straight to them and saved a lot of time in the saddle. The trip would have been shorter, and we would have been spared a lot of wear and tear on our bodies. However, because we had no guide to point us to the cows, we had no choice but to go looking ourselves.

God is our guide through the problems that challenge us in our lives. Because we know he is there to guide us, our view of our problems changes. We have the resources of the God of all creation on our side. He has promised to provide for us and care for us. Doesn't it make sense to ask for his help as we place our worries at his feet? With God's guidance, we need to do what we can to resolve our problems and to change those things we can change. But we have to recognize our limitations and put all our challenges into God's hands.

Next time you find yourself worrying, read the words of Christ as they were recorded in Luke 12:22-26: "Therefore I tell you, do not worry about your life, what you will eat; or about your body, what you will wear. Life is more than food, and the body more than clothes. Consider the ravens: They do not sow or reap, they have no storeroom or barn; yet God feeds them. And how much more valuable you are than birds! Who of you by worrying can add a single hour to his life? Since you cannot do this very little thing, why do you worry about the rest?"

After reading that passage, ponder its meaning.

WITNESSING IS EASY

When people used to talk to me about witnessing for the Lord, I immediately got a mental picture of going house to house and knocking on doors to hand out flyers. Although this kind of witnessing is appropriate in some instances, there are simpler things we can do every day to let people know about the Lord and the good news of the gospel.

To start with, as a Christian, your life is a witness. As people get to know you and see your life, doors of opportunity for talking about what you believe will open.

One day a man came to our house to repair our water heater. A chance to witness? As it turned out, my wife and I witnessed to this man without much effort at all. As he sat in our kitchen, writing up the bill, he casually asked, "You have all this religious stuff in your house. What church do you attend?" We told him about our church and a little about what we believe. He then explained that several people had been talking to him about religion. He wasn't sure what to believe. We talked for quite a while and even loaned him a book to read. A water heater repair call may not seem to be the ideal time to witness, yet the opportunity was there.

Actually, our lives are full of opportunities. Many people ask me questions about religion simply because they know I go to church. Or people find out that Ruth is the choir director or that I sing in the choir. Then it's easy to invite them to come to church and hear us sing. A church newsletter lying around the house can open up an opportunity to invite guests to church or a church activity. Special occasions at church are great times to invite people. If someone is singing or serving as a narrator for a special service, that presents a wonderful opportunity to invite others to church. People love to see kids sing. Anytime your children are involved in a worship service is a good time to invite their friends to visit the church. Church social activities provide opportunities for guests to get to know some of the members of your congregation. This will help them feel less intimidated the first time they walk into church for a service. Christian music playing on the car or home stereo can also spark a conversation about what we believe.

Our job is to tell others about the hope that is in our hearts through Christ and to offer others opportunities to hear God's Word. The Holy Spirit does the work in their hearts. Although nothing may seem to come of your witnessing, don't be too sure. The Holy Spirit works in his own time frame. Be patient. Be helpful. We don't need to argue or push, but just tell others what Jesus has done for us. "Be prepared to give an answer to everyone who asks you to give the reason for the hope that you have" (1 Peter 3:15). The reason for our hope is simple: Jesus died for our sins and rose again from the dead. People will come when the Holy Spirit creates a hunger for that hope in their hearts.

Let us pray every day for opportunities to witness and for the ability to recognize and make use of those opportunities when they occur. Let us pray that the Holy Spirit will work through our words to bring others to know the everlasting hope that is theirs also through Christ.

THERE'S NOTHING TO IT!

Once during the calving season, I offered my rancher friend a helping hand. Well over a hundred cows and heifers were due to calve any day. Since I had helped him on many other occasions, I should have been suspicious as soon as I heard him say, "There's nothing to it!"

The plan did sound simple enough. We would drive out into the pasture with feed for the cows, and then we would check for new calves. Whenever we found one, we would vaccinate it, give it medicine for scours, and attach a tag to its right ear.

As soon as we were done feeding the cows, we began to look for untagged calves. We found the first one standing close to its mother in the middle of the feeding herd. With the syringe in his shirt pocket and the whip in his hand, my friend swung down out of the pickup. "Grab the ear-tagging pliers and follow me," he directed. "Watch. There's nothing to it!"

What happened in the next two minutes was a sight to see. As soon as he took one step toward the calf, the mother's radar went from standby to full alert. He straddled the calf, and clamped its head between his legs. One hand held the calf's muzzle. The other held the whip. The cow got a bead on the stranger who was attacking her newborn calf. Letting loose with a bellow that stopped the other cows in midswallow, she headed straight for him. In an attempt to dissuade the cow from knocking him over, the rancher cracked the whip. She stopped, dodged right, then left, then backed up and nervously stepped forward. She wouldn't stand quietly by as a man apparently tried to hurt her baby. Of course all the commotion attracted several other cows that wanted ringside seats for the main event.

My friend yelled for me to bring the shovel and to hit her with it if I had to in order to keep her away. I returned to find at least six cows, poised just two feet from my friend, seemingly waiting for the okay to bowl him over. Using the flat of the shovel to get them out of the way, I was finally able to get between the rancher and the cows, and we were finally able to vaccinate and tag the calf.

"I haven't had one like that all year," my friend admitted.

So much for "There's nothing to it," I thought to myself.

Being a Christian is like working with those calves. Usually, in America, it is pretty easy. We are free to go to church at will. We have nice church buildings, and the Lord has provided knowledgeable pastors. And as we go about our regular Sunday worship routine, we may appear, on the outside, to be good examples of what Christians should be. But are we? What about when something unexpected happens? What do we do when a spouse or child has no interest in the church and may resent the time we spend there and the offerings we give? Or when an opportunity comes up to do something else on Sunday mornings? What about when friends or jobs keep us from serving our Lord? What if our church facility is rather humble and perhaps even needs repair? Will we be ashamed to attend? What if our personality clashes with a prominent member of the congregation?

My friend the cattle rancher could have thought of a hundred reasons to pass on working with a calf whose angry mother was snorting in his face. But it is precisely in doing what should be done that a person shows the strength of his or her convictions.

Are we willing to put everything on the line for Christ? Are his work and his church our main priorities, or do they get what is left over from our difficult and busy schedules? Are our priorities straight, or are those difficult "cows" psyching us out and causing us to listen to the voice of the sinful nature as it seductively invites us to take the easy way out? If these questions cause us to hang our heads in shame, then let us go to the Lord in repentance. As we remember him hanging on the cross, may we know that he paid for these sins too and that he remembers our sins no more.

Let us pray that the Lord will give us wisdom, energy, and strength to establish the right priorities in our lives. May our priorities reflect the wisdom of the inspired writer who encourages us: "Let us throw off everything that hinders and the sin that so easily entangles, and let us run with perseverance the race marked out for us. Let us fix our eyes on Jesus, the author and perfecter of our faith, who for the joy set before him endured the cross, scorning its shame, and sat down at the right hand of the throne of God. Consider him who endured such opposition from sinful men, so that you will not grow weary and lose heart" (Hebrews 12:1-3).

As we make decisions and plans, as we set priorities and schedules, may we fix our eyes always on Jesus.

Where Are the Role Models?

Have you ever stopped to think about how American culture has changed over the last century? Compare the fashions of the early twentieth century, the twenties and thirties, the fifties and sixties, and today. Have they changed? Don't you think members of previous generations would have been arrested for wearing the kinds of swimsuits worn today?

Compare the language considered acceptable in the early 1900s with language commonly used today. When I was still teaching, I heard language that would turn a sailor's ears blue. I never allowed such language in my classroom, but I didn't seem to have much impact on the language outside the classroom. How about the language in some movies? Apparently some screenwriters have chosen to limit the script to words that are mainly four letters long—and that don't spell l-o-v-e.

Except for late at night or on movie channels, TV programming is supposed to be suitable for the family. But have you noticed how programmers have pushed the limits on subject matter? Discrimination against family values is the norm. In their place the values expressed promote adultery, homosexuality, and general disregard for marriage vows and the institution of marriage itself. Inevitably, the programs glorify people who represent godless religions and make light of those who express the will of the true God. Dysfunctional family situations become the focus of comedy routines. Offbeat entertainers and undisciplined sports figures not only receive positive press coverage but are elevated as role models for our children. Pastors, on the other hand, are presented as weak, ineffectual, or extreme. Sex out of marriage and kids born out of wedlock are accepted. Marriage, if the subject is dealt with at all, seldom expresses a healthy relationship. Abortion is generally accepted. Those who oppose it are portrayed as ultraconservative weirdoes. From TV we might draw the following conclusions: Teenagers are disrespectful and their lack of respect should be worn as a badge of honor. They are often violent, always in trouble, and usually in gangs. Violence is the preferred method for solving problems. Hunters and gun owners are shown to use firearms illegally. Organizations that actually promote the responsible use of guns are portrayed as somehow to blame when a misguided person kills students at a high school. All politicians are crooked and trying to put one over on taxpayers. Police are quite often corrupt. Businesses are willing to make a buck at any cost because money, of course, is the answer to everything.

Whatever happened to *Father Knows Best, Ozzie and Harriet, Red Skelton,* and *Gunsmoke?* Where are the role models?

You and I are role models to our neighbors, our children, and our brothers and sisters in our churches. Not models of perfection certainly. But we are models of sinners who cherish the forgiveness won for us in Christ and who, in that forgiveness, find the strength to demonstrate kindness, honesty, charity, and love for one another—all to the glory of God. We can show by example that TV's gloomy picture of the world doesn't have to be our world. We don't need to covet and steal, because God has promised that he will provide. We aren't overcome with a feeling of emptiness that drives us to try to find meaning at the bottom of a bottle or in an illicit relationship. We know that in Christ our lives have eternal meaning and purpose.

Jesus tells his disciples of all time, "Let your light shine before men, that they may see your good deeds and praise your Father in heaven" (Matthew 5:16). What a remarkable privilege God has given to us, to reflect his light to the world through our lives! May God use us to shine the light of truth and hope to our sin-darkened world.

LET'S NOT GIVE
THE BIBLE BACK!

One of Ruth's pet complaints is that I always leave books lying around the house where they get in the way. She keeps telling me to return the borrowed books to their owners and to find homes for the rest.

I admit I have a "few" books around for keepsakes. Eight or ten bookcases full really aren't all that many. I also admit that, at any given time, I will be reading six or eight books on a variety of topics, and I often let them lie around so they will always be handy. I keep some by the bed, some by my easy chair, some in the kitchen, some in the bathroom, and some in a few other miscellaneous spots around the house. I wouldn't describe them as "in the way." Which book I choose to read on a particular day depends on my mood.

It's true some of the books, including the borrowed ones, tend to get "lost" on some more obscure shelves or in other hiding places. I agree I should get them back to their owners if I am not using them. Therefore, to keep the peace, when Ruth presses me about the books, I always tell her I plan to organize them and return those I've borrowed "tomorrow"! Sometimes, I actually intend to do so. The catch, of course, is that "tomorrow" rarely comes.

This discussion about returning books to their owners takes my mind back to my childhood. When I visited homes as a kid, I would often see Bibles. It always struck me as odd that, in several of those homes, the Bible would be in the same place week after week. Sometimes fancy expensive Bibles were prominently displayed, apparently for people to notice. However, they never seemed to be actually used. They just stayed in one place and collected dust.

As I have grown older, I understand why. My own study of God's Word often gets put on the back burner. It's easy for me to put TV, skiing, sports, work, nap time, the honey-do list, and a host of other things ahead of reading my Bible. Then I find myself thinking, *When was the last time I sat down and really studied God's book?* Now and then the thought crosses my mind that I could just as well return the book to its owner for all the use I was getting out of it. No matter how unique the Bible may be, or how elaborate the display, if we just leave the Bible on a book-shelf or coffee table, we get nothing out of it. (Putting it under your pillow at night in the hope that you will absorb the contents by osmosis doesn't work either. I know. I tried that with some of my textbooks in college. No luck!)

When we get so carried away with life that our Bible reading lags, we miss some very special blessings that God intends to give us.

The Bible is God's book. The words are his words. He doesn't want the book back. He wants us to keep it, study it, understand it, ponder it, and receive its blessings. "[God's] word is a lamp to my feet and a light for my path," the psalmist tells us (Psalm 119:105). He recognized the blessings that God's Word brings to us. He knew that God's Word guides us on the path of life.

"From infancy you have known the holy Scriptures, which are able to make you wise for salvation through faith in Christ Jesus," Paul told Timothy (2 Timothy 3:15). Paul knew that the one thing which sets us free when the guilt of the things we have done wrong threatens to suffocate us is the promise of forgiveness through Jesus. That message is established by the Word of God.

"You have been born again, not of perishable seed, but of imperishable, through the living and enduring word of God," Peter wrote (1 Peter 1:23). He knew that God's Word is not simply the source of wisdom, it makes us alive—eternally.

I know that those of us who have been church members a long time take our Bibles for granted. We begin to think we have heard all the Bible stories so many times that there is nothing more for us to learn. But the more we study, the more we realize we have just begun to mine the precious treasures that glisten from the pages of God's Word. As we learn to recognize those precious treasures, we will never allow our Bibles to collect dust again. Instead, the Bible will become our most used book.

SUNDAY: A DAY OF OPPORTUNITIES

Have you ever stopped and asked yourself, "Why do I go to a church service on Sunday morning?" Perhaps you come to worship, hear the Word, confirm your need for forgiveness, ask for forgiveness for your sins, or give praise to God. Perhaps you've been doing these things since childhood. It's become a habit. Perhaps you enjoy talking with the people. You cherish the encouragement you receive from other Christians.

All of these are important reasons for attending church. We all need to hear regularly that our sins are forgiven. We need to be reminded that we can trust God as he works for our good in our lives. We certainly can benefit from the message the pastor has spent hours preparing. And we treasure the opportunities to give thanks, to enjoy Christian fellowship, and to reap encouragement as we gather together with our brothers and sisters in Christ.

But let's face it. Sometimes we forget how important these opportunities are. We may walk into church thinking, *Let's hurry up and get this duty out of the way* or *I hope this makes my wife, husband, or parent happy.*

I have often found that if I expect to get something out of the service, I have to be willing to put something into it. A church service is a special event during which we are presented with opportunities. We can choose to take advantage of these opportunities or to ignore them. A thought-provoking movie will provoke no thoughts if we don't watch it. An inspiring book will not inspire if we don't read it. A song brings joy to none if no one listens. If we are to benefit from the opportunities offered in our worship services, we have to make use of those opportunities. Sometimes it requires a bit of effort on our part to keep our minds focused.

Bible study with our brothers and sisters in Christ is another opportunity that many congregations offer in addition to worship services. There we are able to study a portion of the Word in greater depth as we feed our Christian faith.

Feeding our Christian faith is very important. If we carefully plant a seed in a pot filled with good soil and give it plenty of water, it will grow well in the sunlight. That is, it will grow well as long as it continues to get sunlight, water, and fertilizer. If we stop providing those important ingredients for a short time, the plant will be stunted. If we stop long enough, the plant will die. Our Christian faith is much like that plant. In fact, the Bible often uses water and light as pictures of the life-giving message of Jesus found in the Word. "Whoever is thirsty, let him come; and whoever wishes, let him take the free gift of the water of life" (Revelation 22:17). "[Jesus] said, 'I am the light of the world. Whoever follows me will never walk in darkness, but will have the light of life'" (John 8:12). Our faith needs the constant nourishment of the Word. Yes, we can read the Bible at home or at work. We will be blessed if we do that. But as we also study with our fellow Christians, our pastor is able to teach us things we wouldn't have picked up from our private reading. And we benefit from the questions of others, questions we might not have thought of on our own.

Sundays are truly days of opportunity, as we attend church services and Bible studies. Let's make use of these precious opportunities. And may God bless us as we drink the water of life that flows from his Word!

THE WORD WILL NOT RETURN EMPTY

Sometimes we get discouraged when our church membership doesn't grow as fast as we had hoped. We wring our hands and say, "We just don't know what else we can do to improve our outreach." However, we must always remember the words our Lord speaks to us through his prophet: "So is my word that goes out from my mouth: It will not return to me empty, but will accomplish what I desire and achieve the purpose for which I sent it" (Isaiah 55:11). He asks us to faithfully proclaim his Word, and he promises that his Word will not return empty. We may not always see the results we expected, at least according to our timetables. The Lord is working according to his own timetable.

About 85 percent of the population of Indonesia is Muslim. Less than 10 percent is Christian. Yet, in spite of severe restrictions against sharing the Christian faith, the Word is bearing abundant fruit. Here in the USA, we are able to use the mail to distribute invitations to worship, or we can invite as we canvass from door to door. We can gather in homes to study the Bible or to discuss topics of Christian concern. We can talk to our friends who may not know about the gift of life Jesus offers to them. In Indonesia these things are illegal. That's right, illegal. Only registered church buildings can be used as Christian meeting places. Even starting a conversation about Christianity with a prospect is illegal unless they ask about it first. Advertising is only allowed from established churches. Christian missionaries are not allowed into the country except as theological experts. That means they can only work to instruct the native Christian leaders. They are not allowed to start churches or work with the general Indonesian population.

As I was listening to a 28-year-old Lutheran elementary school teacher speak about the two years she spent teaching in Indonesia, I thought to myself, *What is the point? How can God's Word possibly be making any headway in a land with so many restrictions on the teaching of the Bible?* So I asked her point-blank if she felt the church was growing in Indonesia. Without hesitation, she assured me that it was. She explained that God provides ways to witness in spite of the restrictions. For example, she indicated she had been able to speak of God's Word in her school classes.

Throughout history, people have often tried to restrict the spread of the message of Jesus. The good news has spread in spite of the restrictions. Think of the persecution of the early Christians. Though the persecution was sometimes horrible, the number of Christians continued to grow as the message of life spread throughout the world.

The time may come when Christians will be persecuted in this country also. But right now doors of opportunity are open. Let's go through those doors. Let's use those opportunities. Why should we get discouraged and complain? God works wherever his Word is preached and taught. Our job is to present the message of life everlasting. The rest we must leave to the Lord. We can't afford to be discouraged, nor can we delay. And we need not doubt that God will accomplish great things through his Word.

Our Children Learn from Us

Parents sometimes forget how much they influence their children's spiritual growth, and how important that influence is. My folks always made sure my sister, my brother, and I made it to Sunday school, though I can honestly say I didn't always want to go. As a kid I could think of any number of things that were more important, like horseback riding, hiking, hunting, or watching TV. Yes, even watching TV.

Those who have been around a while remember how important that first TV was. For months our family lived off of TV trays in front of that first 21-inch black and white tube. Though I could easily come up with what I thought were valid reasons for missing Sunday school, my folks always stressed that those things came second.

As I look back almost half a century later, I am thankful they didn't take the easy way out and let me stay home. Because of their quiet expectation that Sundays would be spent listening to God, he had an opportunity to work in my heart. Some of the fondest and most life-changing memories of my childhood revolve around the dedicated group of people who took the time and interest to represent Christ to me. Yet, in many cases, I would have chosen not to participate if my parents hadn't insisted.

Words can't adequately express how much those basic lessons have meant to me over the years. Though at one point in my life, I thought I was too busy to hear God's Word regularly, I eventually caught on to what was missing in my life. I'm eternally thankful that my parents understood how important it was that I heard God's Word.

Where will our children be 30, 40, or 50 years from now? Where they end up then depends a lot on where they start today. Let's make sure they start at the foot of the cross. Let us show them that hearing God's Word is our highest priority—and theirs.

"Train a child in the way he should go, and when he is old he will not turn from it" (Proverbs 22:6).

HURRAH FOR THE MOVIES!

They just don't make movies like they used to. While my wife and I were sitting at the dinner table recently, I turned on the TV. *Lilies of the Field,* a movie that earned Sidney Poitier an academy award for best actor, was playing. What a great little film! I believe that film should be required watching for any church considering a building project. The story revolves around the actions of several German nuns who have arrived in the American Southwest. Against all odds, they convince Poitier's character to help them build a chapel. It is funny and cute and interjects a powerful message that God's work will get done, no matter what forces work against it. I haven't witnessed that kind of message in many movies lately.

Think about it. Movies mirror our society or, at least, our perceptions of society. That same evening after we watched *Lilies of the Field,* I read an article about the movies that had just been nominated for academy awards that year. The movie topics included death row, the tormented souls of the dead, a combination orphanage and abortion mill, a boy from a broken home who could see ghosts, the bonds between prison guards and condemned criminals, and a tobacco industry whistle-blower. Male characters included a father who blackmails his boss, smokes pot with a neighbor kid, and spends time flirting with some of his daughter's cheerleading friends. Female characters included one with a sexual identity crisis, two who were adulterous wives, and several who were struggling single moms. What does this selection of films say about us as a society? What kind of example do these films set for those who watch them? Is there a message in these films and, if so, is it one we want or need to hear? What are they saying to our children?

Sin is habit forming. One act sets the stage for another a little further over the line. When we support one film that's just a little beyond our comfort zone, the next may take us one step further. And I am as guilty as anyone. I love movies. I have a number in my collection to prove it. However, I have been known to refuse to go see certain ones. I have also returned some videos that looked good on the cover but were downright ugly on the screen.

In 1 Corinthians 5:6, Paul asked, "Don't you know that a little yeast works through the whole batch of dough?" We need to use good Christian sense in our viewing habits. Just as "a little yeast works through the whole batch of dough," so the images of immorality, the occult, violence, and perversion that bombard our minds may dull our sense of what is good and right.

We also have the opportunity to set an example for others, especially our children. As we explain why we don't want to watch certain shows or support certain programs, others may ask themselves whether their choices glorify God. Let's support and say hurrah for those programs and films we find worthwhile. If we support the good ones and avoid the bad ones, the moviemakers will notice. Perhaps we will see some wholesome movies again.

Then I can hope to see you at the movies!

If You Are Not Happy with Your Work, Read This

Many people must get up each day and work at a job they hate. It seems almost every time I am around others, I hear people complain that this or that is wrong with their lot in life. She doesn't want to do housework. His boss isn't fair. Work hours are too long. The work is too difficult, boring, unsatisfying, or pointless. Coworkers are irritating. The pay is not high enough. It's hard to find a place to park. People would rather be doing something else. I have even heard retired folks complain that they never get a day off—they are busier than when they were working at a regular job.

I would like to introduce you to two people I know. They have changed my attitude about my work, both at home and on the job. They might change your attitude too.

One of my teachers is a mechanic. I once had to ask him to come over on his day off to repair a vehicle that belonged to a friend who was visiting our home. I noticed especially this mechanic's attitude toward his work. As he fixed the engine, he mentioned that he loved what he did. I guess I sort of looked at him expecting him to mention some exceptions, but he never did. Instead, he explained that he enjoyed having the opportunity to help people and that he looked forward to coming to work each day. He felt that the Lord had blessed him by leading him to a job he really enjoyed.

My wife and I see this mechanic and his wonderful family in church almost every Sunday. It is apparent to everyone that they both love what they are doing. Every time I see them, I think about what he said about his job and what a wonderful Christian attitude they have toward their work.

My second teacher cleans houses for a living. Not many people consider housekeeping to be fun. Given a choice, I and many others would avoid it entirely. So one day as I was talking with my housekeeper, I expressed my appreciation for her work, especially because I disliked housekeeping so much. Her reply made me rethink my own feelings about the things I do each day. She said, "No matter where the Lord puts me, I believe he put me there for a reason. So I enjoy doing housework because I do it for him. It is as if the house I am cleaning is his house." She went on to quote Colossians 3:23: "Whatever you do, work at it with all your heart, as working for the Lord, not for men." She told me that she once worked in a factory. All day long she worked putting nuts onto bolts. She enjoyed the work because she felt she was there for the Lord. Though to me, putting nuts on bolts all day long would be very boring, she didn't see it that way. She felt that job was God's will for her at that point in time. And because she had faith that God wanted her to do the best possible job, she even worked out ways of doing the job faster and more efficiently.

We know that in everything God works for the good of those who love him. We can be sure of that because through Jesus' life, death, and resurrection, we have been brought into the family of God. Through our faithful, honest labor, we thank God for the great gift he has given us. So, in a sense, we are working for God. Even if we don't fully understand why we have a certain job, we are happy to give glory to God through our work. Whether we are housekeepers or highly paid professionals, if we see our jobs as means to glorify God, our attitude about our work will change.

DAD

Where does a young boy learn the values that will be the foundation for his life when he becomes an adult? Many places, but often from his dad.

My dad stood six feet tall and weighed 185 pounds. He made his living as a rancher, raising citrus fruit, avocados, and cattle. Though he worked outside all the time and was about as rugged and tough as they come, he was also a soft-spoken family man, a loving husband, and a Christian.

One day during my high school years, as we were putting gas into the old work truck, he looked right at me and said, "If you ever feel you have to steal something, come and ask me. I'll give it to you." Having been a teenager once himself, I guess he thought that a teenager like me might get tempted. I wasn't, but what he said always stayed with me. I knew that he understood what it meant to be a kid. I also understood that he didn't want me to do something stupid that would burden my conscience for the rest of my life.

Dad loved horses, cattle, citrus trees, good values, and hard work. Boy, did he like hard work! He put in many long days managing his father's ranch and then would come home and work on his own small ranch. Though record keeping was not his strong suit, honesty and fairness were all-important to him. Nothing upset him more quickly than dishonesty or unfairness.

He also had a sense of humor—even when the joke cost him a lot of time and effort. I'll never forget the time the man who was trucking fruit out of the orchard told Dad he had backed into a concrete irrigation stand. He assured Dad that the irrigation stand wasn't broken, just loose. Of course, Dad knew that the concrete pipe was broken several feet underground and he would have to dig a huge hole to fix it. However, he laughed every time he repeated that story because he knew the man honestly thought he hadn't done any real damage. "It's not broken, just loose!" still makes me smile.

Dad cherished his family. He loved my mother with all his heart. Mom was not strong and suffered from a series of illnesses throughout their married life. But Dad rarely complained. He often came home during the day to check on her and regularly helped with many of the household chores. And when our family eventually grew to include three kids, Dad spent time with each of us. He always took pride in the things we did well, and he was always there when we needed a little push or someone to listen.

Church was important to both Mom and Dad. They made sure we kids got to Sunday school and church regularly. When we received awards for attendance and memory work, they were proud. And they showed an interest in what we studied.

A trumpet player during his school years, Dad always loved music and especially enjoyed Herb Alpert and the Tijuana Brass. He also loved to hear me play trumpet for school or church. Never complaining when I practiced, he always encouraged me to do more.

He also encouraged me to go to college even though he had to borrow against the ranch to help pay for my education. But he did that quietly. I didn't even know about it until I found the loan papers after he died.

One of the most difficult challenges of my life was to watch this once strong man slowly weaken. In 1971 he began having such serious back trouble that it hurt him to bend over to move the sprinkler hoses. Being a jack-of-all-trades he devised a hook on a pole to help him move the hoses without having to bend over. His hands got so numb, from what was diagnosed as carpal tunnel syndrome, that he could no longer get his jackknife from his pocket. Not long after the last of several operations to correct the pinched nerves, the doctors discovered the real culprit. He had multiple myeloma, a deadly form of bone cancer. There was no cure, and the "hot pills," as Dad liked to call his chemotherapy, only slowed the disease a little. Because the chemotherapy made him hold water, he eventually ended up taking handfuls of diuretics. But he never complained—and he continued to work until just a few weeks before he died.

He also continued to find comfort in his daily devotions, as he had for so many years. He appreciated his minister's regular visits and the reassurance from God's Word. As the end drew near, the whole family came home to visit him. We saw, even more clearly than before, the truth of Jesus' words that there is one thing that is needful.

Dad died on a Monday morning in his own bed, at the ranch he loved, with my mother at his side. He was 56.

I thank God that I had a father who taught me so much about life. He left behind a wonderful legacy of love for God, his family, nature, hard work, honesty, and humor. I pray that I will always follow in the footsteps of his faith.

"These commandments that I give you today are to be upon your hearts. Impress them on your children. Talk about them when you sit at home and when you walk along the road, when you lie down and when you get up" (Deuteronomy 6:6,7).

THE GRADUATION GIFT

In 1960 I graduated from high school in Fillmore, California. Like most graduates, I received some gifts. Most I have long since worn out, spent, or forgotten, but one prized possession still remains—a copy of the Amplified New Testament, given to me by a distant cousin, Dwight, and his wife.

Dwight taught Sunday school and led our church singing. Always upbeat, he especially enjoyed working with young people. And we especially enjoyed it when Dwight and La Rue hosted our Sunday evening youth gatherings. At their home, we knew we were in for a good time. As he led the devotion and spirited singing, Dwight took it upon himself to set a Christian example for young people to follow. We, in turn, really liked and respected him.

I still remember the night he taught us about giving of our time, talents, and wealth. With complete sincerity, he taught that God comes first in our lives. I often think about what Dwight taught, especially when I am tempted to say no to opportunities to use my time, money, or effort to serve the Lord in his church.

Think about it. Even as Jesus prayed in the Garden of Gethsemane, he knew that his betrayer was coming with a makeshift posse to arrest him and to kill him. When faced with the choice of escaping or walking the path of suffering, Jesus put us first so that we might have life. He freed us from a life of serving our own selfishness, so that we are able to put God first.

Dwight's graduation gift was special, not just because it came from him but because of the simple inscription he wrote inside: "Graduation congratulations! from Dwight and LaRue. Romans 10:9,10,11. Romans 8:28 (These are good verses to remember)."

I've pondered those words many times since my graduation. "If you confess with your mouth, 'Jesus is Lord,' and believe in your heart that God raised him from the dead, you will be saved. For it is with your heart that you believe and are justified, and it is with your mouth that you confess and are saved. As the Scripture says, 'Anyone who trusts in him will never be put to shame'" (Romans 10:9-11). "And we know that in all things God works for the good of those who love him, who have been called according to his purpose" (Romans 8:28).

What great thoughts for life's many graduations.

Yes. We go through many stages of change in our lives. I'm thankful Dwight was willing to spend so much time with us to remind us to take God's Word with us as we go through these times of change.

The importance of the things Dwight taught us was brought home to me not long after I left Fillmore. I received word that Dwight had been killed. His dump truck rolled back, toppled over a bank, and pinned him underneath.

He was a real inspiration to many of us. I think God is talking about people like him when he urges us: "Remember your leaders, who spoke the word of God to you. Consider the outcome of their way of life and imitate their faith" (Hebrews 13:7).

ONE WORRIED ROBIN

One morning at early dawn, a loud thud woke me from my sleep. Something had hit one of our living room windows. Though ordinarily I would have gone to investigate, that morning I didn't even open my eyes. I knew what it was. You see, a robin lives in the trees not far from our window, and he's a worrier. When it gets light, he sees his reflection in the window and thinks that another robin is about to take over his territory. The closer he moves toward the "usurper," the closer the image appears in the window. He spends hours working himself into a frenzy and beating himself against the window. If he would only understand that things are not as bad as they seem—he really is the imagined problem—he would have a much nicer day. Maybe he would avoid eventually hurting himself.

Most of the time things are not as bad as they seem. What happens to us may not be what we would want or like to happen, but it usually isn't as bad as we imagined. How many times haven't we spent days worrying about something, only to find that it wasn't worth the worry? In our eyes, life has a way of appearing just like the world must appear to our misguided robin. We see our little world through our human eyes. We worry and worry about what we think we see. We forget that God works through all things for the good of those who love him.

Paul tells us: "Do not be anxious about anything, but in everything, by prayer and petition, with thanksgiving, present your requests to God. And the peace of God, which transcends all understanding, will guard your hearts and your minds in Christ Jesus" (Philippians 4:6,7). Instead of anxiety, we can have peace as we place our challenges into the hands of our all-powerful and all-wise God. We can have peace because we know he cares for us. And we know that he has the power to do all things for our good.

Christ himself said: "Are not two sparrows sold for a penny? Yet not one of them will fall to the ground apart from the will of your Father. And even the very hairs of your head are all numbered. So don't be afraid; you are worth more than many sparrows" (Matthew 10:29-31). If we worry, it is as though we don't believe that God cares about us or knows what is happening to us. But he knows even how many hairs we have on our heads. He knows when a sparrow falls. And we are worth much more than the sparrows. We don't need to beat ourselves up with worry the way that robin did.

May God show us that we can pray more and worry less!

I REMEMBER THE
RAINBOW'S PROMISE

I never grow tired of exploring the wonders of nature, which God has so freely provided for us all. I still remember one special trip.

We arose early from our sleeping bags, loaded our packs, and saddled our horses. After a hearty breakfast of bacon, toast, eggs, and pancakes, our expedition began. My grandfather, three friends, three guides, a horse wrangler, and I were on a pack trip and big game hunt in a remote area of British Columbia.

The trip was both exhilarating and challenging. The late August air felt brisk against our faces, as nine riders guided nine saddle horses, several colts, and seven pack horses across an alfalfa field toward the base of a ridge. From there we followed a meandering trail as it wound its way up fog-shrouded hills. All morning we worked our way higher and deeper into the wild mysterious beauty of the Shoelap Mountains. We had to pause often, either to rest after a steep climb or to let the guide's chain saw do its work. Because this trail hadn't been used since the previous winter, many windfalls had to be cleared. On one occasion, ground bees sent a passing pack animal bucking wildly off the trail, strewing equipment, including the chain saw, in all directions.

As we climbed a high ridge that led to our first campsite, a summer shower drenched the area. Then, as quickly as the clouds had appeared, they parted. The remaining mist formed millions of tiny prisms that bent the sun's rays into a breathtaking double rainbow. We paused, gazing in awe at this glorious symbol of God's workmanship and promise.

God's workmanship had been visible everywhere we looked. We had seen it in the glowing fires of the sunrise and the collage of bright sunlight and dark shadows that defined the deep forest. We had sensed it in the sweet aroma of the spring-irrigated alfalfa field. And now, from this high vantage point, his handiwork shown brightly through the mists in the form of this large rainbow—the largest I had ever seen.

In the days ahead, we would see countless other evidences of God's glorious work—snowcapped peaks, graceful wildlife, and clear, blue mountain lakes. We felt the joy and exhilaration of trekking through a part of God's creation that had been little touched by the hand of man. But etched in my mind will always be that double rainbow, so large it took two photos to capture its full length. The memory of that glorious symbol of God's promise never to send another universal flood will always be, for me, a comforting reminder of God's continuing presence and power and of his love for each of us.

"Whenever the rainbow appears in the clouds, I will see it and remember the everlasting covenant between God and all living creatures of every kind on the earth" (Genesis 9:16).

THE BLESSINGS
OF CHRISTIAN SUPPORT

My mother went to be with her Lord on September 14, 2001. Having been ill for many years, she had needed help of one kind or another during the 26 years since my father had died. After my sister and her family helped Mother for 16 years in California, she spent 6 years with my brother's family in Colville, Washington. Due to failing health, she spent the last three and a half years of her life near my wife and me in Yakima area adult family homes.

She knew very few people in Yakima—life in an adult family home is not conducive to meeting a lot of people. She did, however, find an accepting family in our church.

Though she had been a Christian most of her life, she had not been raised in the Lutheran church. At my request, Pastor Franck began to visit her when she first arrived. Later Pastor Westra continued to work with her. It took some time, but Mother finally professed her faith, and her desire to become a member of Redeemer Lutheran Church.

She had many physical problems, including advanced arthritis, failing eyesight, pinched nerves that caused chronic numbness in her hands, and nearly unbearable headaches. More than half of her stomach had been removed, and her feet and ankles were too weak and painful to support her weight. However, in spite of her handicaps, she came to church and Bible study whenever she could.

I still feel profound gratitude to all the members of Redeemer Lutheran Church who supported her in so many ways. Several visited her regularly in the adult family home. The pastors served her faithfully by bringing her the Word and Sacrament in her room. Many took the time to stop and chat with her when she was able to attend church. Even though she had trouble hearing, and people had trouble understanding her, many congregation members worked hard to make her feel wanted. The ushers and other volunteers were there to help get her up and down the stairs and sometimes joke with her a little in the process. At the coffee hours, caring people always made sure she had company, coffee, and food. A group from church that went to breakfast most Sunday mornings included her in those gatherings. When she was not in church, she received her church newsletter and bulletins thanks to another family—how she loved getting mail! All of these Christian people reached out to her in a meaningful way and made her feel at home. In fact, about a week before she died, she told me that she hoped she could get well enough to go to church again.

When Mother passed away, Ruth and I felt the full Christian support of Redeemer's members. Countless visits and words of condolence lifted us up. God's Word at the memorial service offered spiritual salve for our wounded hearts. The generosity of those who printed the funeral folder, offered their musical skills for the service, gave cards with comforting Christian messages and memorials in her name, worked hard preparing for the fellowship luncheon, phoned with uplifting messages, and volunteered the use of their equipment and pickups—all these expressions of love moved us greatly. I can't even tell you how much all that Christian support from Redeemer meant to us! However, I can tell you that this outpouring of love reaffirmed my belief that God works in special ways when special needs exist. He used the members of Redeemer as a part of the solution.

My mother had marked all the Scripture passages used in the service. Many people told me that the pastor's encouragement from Isaiah 40:29-31 touched their hearts. The little story he used was one my mother and father read together several times just before my father died. The well-worn copy testified that Mother had read the story many times over the years. Mom would have been pleased to know that her memorial service presented God's Word to others in such a meaningful way. How comforting it was for us to hear the wonderful promise that our mother is now free of her pain—she is no longer crippled. Even greater is the promise that because she hoped in the Lord, he would renew her strength, allow her to soar on wings like eagles, run without growing weary, and walk without being faint.

My mother, my extended family, and my friends saw the light of the gospel shining brightly in lives of the members of Redeemer Lutheran Church—during some dark and trying times. We thank the Lord for the comfort he gave through his Word and for the strength he gave through our Christian friends in our time of need.

PRIORITIES
—RURAL KANSAS—
1926

My mother-in-law, Hilda Friebus, shared this story of her early life in Kansas:

In our family, preparations for church started on Saturday. All four of us kids and our parents took turns bathing. Water gathered by means of rain gutters and stored in the cistern beneath the house was hand pumped into the warming compartment on the back of the wood stove or heated on top in kettles. When it was hot, we poured it into the large free-standing bathtub. By evening we all were scrubbed clean, ready to attend church the next morning.

The daylight had barely begun to brighten the sky when we got out of bed on Sunday morning. Everyone had chores before breakfast. The pigs had to be fed. Our 12 cows had to be milked. Then, as someone cranked by hand, the milk was poured through a machine that separated the cream from the milk. Chickens had to be fed, eggs gathered, and breakfast prepared.

When breakfast was ready, Dad said the first part of the common table prayer in German. Then each of us in turn said our personal table prayers. Mine was "The eyes of all wait upon thee; and thou givest them their meat in due season. Thou openest thine hand, and satisfiest the desire of every living thing" (Psalm 145:15,16 King James Version). We were not allowed to leave the table until Dad had finished reading the daily devotion and given thanks using the words of Psalm 106:1 in German.

Finally we would all pile into our Dodge touring car for the eight-mile drive to church in Stuttgart, Kansas. There we would attend Sunday school and the main focus of our Sunday, the worship service.

Even though many things have changed for the better, people often talk about the good old days with tears in their eyes. Perhaps it's because our lives back then weren't quite so full of distractions. People seemed to understand better the things that are really important.

We might do well to renew the focus of our weekends on family devotions, prayer, Bible study and Christian worship. "Remember the Sabbath day by keeping it holy. Six days you shall labor and do all your work, but the seventh day is a Sabbath to the LORD your God" (Exodus 20:8-10). Those words aren't spoken by a stern god who wants to control our lives. Those are words of love from our heavenly Father, who longs to share the glories of heaven with us.

CHRISTMAS EVE—1922

Hilda also shared the following story of a Christmas Eve long ago:

> *Six of us, kids and adults, snuggled warmly under lap robes. The snow was too deep to use our 1916 Dodge touring car for the eight-mile trip to the church in Stuttgart, Kansas, so we were riding in the canvas-covered, two-seat surrey pulled by Jack and Jenny, our two mules. The gas lanterns on the sides of the surrey reflected off the snow, casting eerie shadows. The bells on the harnesses kept a steady rhythm as we rode through the deep snow toward town.*
>
> *We arrived at the church with plenty of time to put the mules in the barn across the street from the church. Because every chair would be used for the Christmas Eve service, we had brought our own. Extras were always needed to seat the two hundred or more worshipers.*
>
> *As we entered the church, we were welcomed by the warmth within. Earlier in the day, the pastor had started a fire in the huge pot-bellied, coal-burning stove located right in the center of the nave. We were glad that he had. The chairs were arranged in neat rows of ten on each side of the center aisle. Children under five were seated with either their fathers or their mothers. Because men and women weren't allowed to*

sit together, the men always sat on the right side of the nave and the women on the left. Children over five were seated in the first three rows followed by the young people, also separated according to gender. The church was lit by a row of large two-mantle, gas lanterns that hung down from the center beam just above the heads of the taller men. Smaller kerosene lamps lined each side wall.

As a typical six-year-old, I was very excited. I had waited, what seemed like forever, for Christmas Eve to arrive. Now at last it was here. I was especially looking forward to the lighting of the 20-foot Christmas tree, which stood to the right side at the front of the church. Because we had no evergreens in Kansas, this tree had been brought in by train from Colorado. An assortment of colored, handblown glass balls covered the tree from top to bottom. At the end of each main branch at the front of the tree, a candleholder had been fastened. It held a narrow, white, three-inch candle. A six-inch wire, with a heavy, inch-and-a-half colored ball attached, extended down from the candleholder. The weight of the ball kept the candle pointed upright. At the very top of the tree, a beautiful white angel reigned over the breathtaking display. Though a few other decorations had been put out, we didn't notice. All eyes were on the tree.

After we took our seats, the candles were lit. Several men with burning candles attached to the ends of sticks lit the higher candles on the tree, while some young boys carefully lit the candles they could reach. As each candle was lit, the light reflected off of the glass balls, making the tree increasingly beautiful. By the time all the candles were lit, the whole front of the church was aglow in a multitude of flickering colors. It *was one of the most beautiful sights my young eyes had ever seen. Two men, seated at each side of the tree, were equipped with water buckets and long sticks with wet clothes wrapped around the end. Their job was to extinguish each candle as it burned low and to put out any fires that might have a chance to start.*

The service was organized and led by our young pastor, but the children did most of the speaking— every child had a piece to say. During the service, various groups of children and young people recited the familiar account of Mary, Joseph, and the babe in the manger. I recited with a group of five. We children also sang several songs, and the congregation sang two as well. The singing was accompanied by a large, reed, pump organ, which sat to the side in the front. It was played by our cheerful organist who had to pump vigorously during the loud parts of each hymn.

As we filed out after the hour-long service was over, each child was handed a plain brown paper bag that contained nuts, candies, and a single orange. We particularly liked the orange—such things were not very common in Kansas.

On our way home in the surrey, we ate candy and talked about the tree, the service, the gifts we expected at home, and, of course, the Christmas service we would attend the next day.

When I grew up, some things were different, of course, than they had been for my mother-in-law. But, it never occurred to us to miss a service either. No matter what the weather. Especially during the Christmas season. Our faith in Christ made our church very much a part of every-day life for my family. Christmastime, with its special church services, was a focal point for the holiday season.

I believe that's the way it should be for every Christian family today. Remember, times have changed, but the Christmas message about the Christ Child and salvation have remained constant.

THE CHRISTMAS TREE

I remember the Christmas trees we had when I was a young kid in the 1940s. Because we lived in southern California, we never had a really big tree. A distant relative always shipped fresh trees from his acreage in Oregon—one for each family within our extended family—but only smaller trees fit into the bicycle boxes he packed them in.

All that made little difference. To us, the fragrance from those little Douglas firs, as my father cut the trunk to fit the tree stand, was the wonderful fragrance of Christmas.

Decorating the tree was a special part of Christmas as well. We used many of the same decorations for our tree each year. The strings of colored lights provided a special challenge because when one bulb went out, the whole string went dark. Then the fun began as we switched bulbs until we found the one that would make them all light up again. A few special lights pointed upward and bubbled with brightly colored liquid. Throughout the branches we carefully placed many shiny colored balls. Somewhere we had found some plastic icicles that glowed from the light they absorbed. We also always bought several ten-cent boxes of silver foil tinsel that glistened in the light. At the top, carefully saved from year to year, a beautiful silver star reigned over our Christmas.

In the evening when the tree was fully decorated and the lights plugged in, it glowed with a subtle beauty that is difficult to describe and is sometimes lost in the glitter of our modern Christmas celebrations. A lot of love was represented in those trees—the love of a family and the love of God for all the world. Sometimes, late on a December night, I can sit in my easy chair, close my eyes, and still see one of those Christmas trees of long ago. Best of all, I can still see the shining Christmas star at the top, telling the world of the coming of the Christ Child. It never fails to give me a sense of wonder and peace.

MY GRANDFATHER'S "SPIRIT OF CHRISTMAS"

Every December, we hear people talk about the "Spirit of Christmas," but I'm not sure many really know what that means. I learned the meaning from my grandfather.

Gramp was a quiet Christian worker who kept the Spirit of Christmas all year-around. Most Sundays he could be found in the inside seat of the last pew at the back of the church. He regularly helped at church picnics, and on several occasions, he went on weeklong trips to work in a mission field. But the Spirit of Christmas was revealed most in the quiet things he did behind the scenes. Without being asked, he selected, bought, and delivered several large sacks of groceries to a desperate family with 11 children. He quietly slipped money for food and rent to the wife of a disabled veteran temporarily out of work. A college student Gramp had never met was working 40 hours a week to support his family. When the student couldn't come up with enough money to complete his degree, Gramp supplied the money. He sponsored another student through a couple of years of college when he found out she would have to drop out for lack of funds. And I can't count how many family members he helped with encouragement, wise counsel, and sometimes material gifts when a hand-up was needed.

In December 1967, a medium-sized, handmade, wooden crate arrived in the mail, with Gramp's name on the return address. When I pried it open, I found inside a miniature, handmade stable to be used with a nativity set. Each piece of wood had been carefully cut, stained with dark walnut stain, and lovingly nailed in its proper place. The design was ingenious. A light shines up through a hole in the roof, illuminating a handmade star, and also down on the baby Jesus. That light reminds us of our twofold job in this world: to let the world know about the newborn Savior and to give all glory to him. That manger scene is still the first decoration I put up and the last I take down.

My grandfather passed away in November of 1977, and I can't tell you how much he is missed. But his Christmas spirit lives on in the work he did. Over the years he quietly made and gave away more than 130 of those stables. In all those homes, the little lights continue to shine on the One who gives meaning to the Spirit of Christmas. The many people who received one of his miniature stables or to whom he offered a helping hand remember a man who understood what it meant to keep the Spirit of Christmas all 365 days of the year.

May God bless us all with the desire to use our talents and our possessions to keep the Spirit of Christmas alive throughout the year. Through our lives, may others always see the one who came to be our Savior.

"So Joseph also went up from the town of Nazareth in Galilee to Judea, to Bethlehem the town of David, because he belonged to the house and line of David. He went there to register with Mary, who was pledged to be married to him and was expecting a child. While they were there, the time came for the baby to be born, and she gave birth to her firstborn, a son. She wrapped him in cloths and placed him in a manger, because there was no room for them in the inn" (Luke 2:4-7).

The Gift

For many of us, buying Christmas gifts is a very special part of a special season. We enjoy the challenge of finding just the right gift for each individual on our list—the thrill of finding something that fits each recipient's personality. Like the hunter who has just bagged a trophy buck, we bask in the sense of accomplishment when we finally hunt down the item he or she really wants. We imagine how our loved ones' eyes will light up with joy and happiness as they open the gifts.

That reminds me of something which happened at a church Christmas party several years ago. Each person brought some goodies to share and a gift to put under the tree. For the gift exchange, we all drew numbers. Whoever drew the number one, got first choice of all the gifts under the tree. However, if the person who held number two liked the gift the first person had opened, he or she could exchange an unopened gift for that one. The obvious catch was that someone on down the line might take the same gift away. This process would continue until all the gifts were claimed.

The evening unfolded into a pleasing display of good fellowship and fun. When it came time for the gift exchange, we were curious, not only to see what we would get but to see who would get the gifts we had put under the tree. I think my contribution was a very nice Gene Autry

Christmas tape I knew someone would be sure to enjoy. Ruth gave a little handmade angel ornament that would be a beautiful addition to someone's Christmas tree. The exchange was punctuated by peals of laughter and howls of consternation whenever someone would help themselves to a gift someone else had already picked.

Ruth and I were both pleased when our pastor's wife picked up Ruth's brightly wrapped contribution. Colleen is a very gracious person. A little shy, she is an extremely sensitive individual who always put the best construction on everything. After she carefully unwrapped the box, she looked inside. A hush settled over the group as everyone waited to see what the box contained. However, instead of immediately producing the gift and thus getting out of the limelight, she hesitated. By the look on her face, we could all see that she was puzzled and a bit embarrassed. Then, she held the box upside down and shook it. Nothing came out. Nothing at all. Searching for the person who gave the box, her eyes scanned the faces around the room.

About then, my mouth dropped open! I was truly speechless. I thought seriously of taking an extended bathroom break. And Ruth turned bright red. She took the box from Colleen and looked inside and shook it herself. Talk about a pregnant pause. Ruth finally recovered her senses enough to try to explain that she must have wrapped the wrong box because there was supposed to be a gift inside. "It was an angel," she stammered, "a sugar-starched, white, crocheted angel. Really!"

Suddenly, absolute silence gave way to uproarious laughter. Colleen's expression had been priceless, as had mine, and especially Ruth's. For the rest of the evening, the whole group got a lot of mileage out of this mistake.

But something striking—somewhat odd, yet profound—resulted from this incident. As the exchange continued, the most popular gift, among a lot of very nice ones, was the empty box. Though the box had been there all along, no one had paid much attention to it until they found that it was empty. Then everyone took notice. Everyone wanted it. One after another, people traded for this gift. The most humble gift in the room, an empty box, became the most valued gift because people believed they would ultimately receive a wonderful gift. Though they didn't really know what that gift would look like, only that it was a crocheted angel, they wanted it because they now believed it was worth having!

The Christmas story is like that. When we get through all the trappings of the Christmas season, all the glitter and expensive presents, we see that the most humble present is the most valuable of all. A child was born in as humble a setting as anyone could imagine, wrapped in strips of cloth, and placed in a manger. Not much to look at on the surface. Yet that child possessed the gift of salvation for us and for the world. Do we understand the full value of this gift? Probably not! Is there some sense of mystery about it? Certainly! But the prophets of Scripture tell us that the gift this humble child brought to the world is the greatest gift we will ever receive. "For to us a child is born, to us a son is given, and the government will be on his shoulders. And he will be called Wonderful Counselor, Mighty God, Everlasting Father, Prince of Peace" (Isaiah 9:6).

That's the mystery and meaning of Christmas. God became one of us in order to bring us peace. Here at the very heart of the Christmas story, sometimes buried deep beneath all the hoopla of the season, is the gift that makes an individual's eyes light up with joy and happiness as no other gift can.

The challenge for you and me during the Christmas season is to extend this great gift to those we know and love. That may not seem to be the fanciest gift, the most expensive, or the largest one. But it is by far the best.

———— • ————

MAYONNAISE AND KETCHUP

Each Christmas season a needy family from the community is assigned to our church. We receive information about the names, ages, and needs of the various children in the family. We try very hard to make sure the children get something for fun and several things they really need such as shoes or coats. We also collect cans and boxes of nonperishable foods. We try to provide plenty of food for several meals in addition to a big Christmas feast.

I have to admit this is one of my pet projects each year. I feel strongly that helping others is one of the ways we reflect the love of Jesus to others. Jesus often spoke of concern for the needy. "When you give a luncheon or dinner, do not invite your friends, your brothers or relatives, or your rich neighbors; if you do, they may invite you back and so you will be repaid. But when you give a banquet, invite the poor, the crippled, the lame, the blind, and you will be blessed. Although they cannot repay you, you will be repaid at the resurrection of the righteous" (Luke 14:12-14). In fact, in Matthew 25:40, Jesus revealed an astounding truth: "I tell you the truth, whatever you did for one of the least of these brothers of mine, you did for me." Many people need a hand up. I needed one when I went through college. Without the work, money, and encouragement several Christians gave me, I would not have made it.

On several occasions, my wife and I have had the privilege of accompanying the pastor when he delivers the gifts. Over the years, the needs of some families have been more evident than others. But one delivery in particular stands out in my mind.

Our assigned family that year included three children. Because of an accident, the father had been unable to work for over a year. The mother had a job, but it was difficult for her to make ends meet. We gathered the boxes of presents our youth group had wrapped, as well as boxes of food items, and called to make sure someone would be home.

With the presents in the back of my pickup, we arrived at the address we had been given. The lady answered the door and invited us to come in. After we introduced ourselves, we presented her with a letter explaining that the gifts were from Redeemer Evangelical Lutheran Church. We also explained a little about what we believe.

The clean living room was decorated with just a few pictures on the wall. A set of crutches stood in one corner. Though it was less than a week before Christmas, the small Christmas tree on the table held only a few handmade decorations. The few presents already under the tree appeared to be handmade. The lady pointed to the portraits of the three children on top of an old television set and proudly told us a little about each of the three boys.

As we placed our presents around the tree, I noticed that the mother was looking at the boxes of food. We began to tell her what was in some of those boxes.

Up to that point I had been fine. The introductions, gift presentation, and discussion about the family hadn't bothered me. However, as we put the last gifts under the tree, she again looked wistfully at the boxes of food. I will never forget what she said as she turned toward us. "I think all I have left in the refrigerator is some mayonnaise and ketchup." Until she said those words, I had not fully recognized their plight. However, as she spoke, something got in my eyes, a lump formed in my throat, and I thanked God our church people had been so generous.

Through James, God tells us "to look after orphans and widows in their distress" (James 1:27). Should Christians be involved in helping the needy? Should we help even more than we do? Should Christians be concerned about the material as well as the spiritual welfare of others? Before you answer, check your refrigerator. How are you fixed for mayonnaise and ketchup?

SURELY NOT I?

The account of Judas' betrayal of Jesus fascinates me. Bible scholars express a variety of opinions why they think Judas did what he did. Some say that he was trying to force Jesus' hand so that he would have to rise up and overthrow the Roman rule. Others say he was simply interested in the 30 pieces of silver. But if his only interest was the money, why did he return it later? The best clue is found in John 13:27: "As soon as Judas took the bread, Satan entered into him." No matter what Judas was thinking at the time, his actions were being governed by Satan.

The fascinating debate over the reason for Judas' betrayal will probably continue as long as the earth remains. However, just as fascinating is the reaction of the rest of the disciples. They clearly did not understand what was happening. When Jesus indicated that one of the Twelve would betray him, they looked around the table at one another and asked, "Surely not I, Lord?" (Matthew 26:22). Even when Judas left to do his dirty work, they didn't get it.

That question, "Surely not I?" won't let go of me. There is something haunting about the question that reaches down into our very souls and begs an answer. Though Judas had already made arrangements to turn Jesus over to the chief priest, even he asked our Lord, "Surely not I?" In my mind's eye I can see the Twelve seated around the table, looking at one another, studying faces, and wondering who the guilty one could possibly be. While their minds and mouths asked the question, "Surely not I?" their hearts may have been wondering, "Is it the one who's sitting right next to me or, perhaps, the one across the table?"

In his account, Luke connects the question of who would betray Jesus to a dispute about who was the greatest among them. Maybe the possibility of betraying Jesus seemed so remote that they started to brag about their loyalty to Jesus. Perhaps, as they tabulated the good things they had done to help his cause, each began to think that he was better than the others.

How often don't we Christians get caught in the same trap in which the disciples found themselves? Though we may not have taken silver and turned Jesus over to be crucified—literally—we are all just as responsible for Christ's crucifixion. We betray Jesus in many ways each day: when we look down on others as though we are better than they are; when we ignore our opportunities to talk to God in prayer; when we neglect his Word by staying away from worship and Bible study; when we withhold the financial gifts God intended us to use to worship him or to help the needy. Each betrayal is another tap on the nails that held Jesus to the cross as he paid the price for our shortcomings.

When our hearts face the question "Are you the one who is betraying Jesus?" we are tempted to look around and ask, "Surely not I?" Instead of admitting our weaknesses and shortcomings, do we try to divert attention by asking, "Is it he? Is it she? Is it the person who lives across the street?" Then, because the devil plays so well on our human nature, we take the next step and start listing all the good things we do. "Look at him or her," we say to ourselves. "Poor excuse for a Christian," we speak judgmentally. "I must really be a great Christian. I can't possibly be guilty of betraying Jesus and causing him to be crucified!"

Wow! By allowing ourselves to think that way, we really miss the point. Jesus quieted the argument very quickly and decisively that night. "The kings of the Gentiles lord it over them; and those who exercise authority over them call themselves Benefactors. But you are not to be like that," he scolded. "Instead, the greatest among you should be like the youngest, and the one who rules like the one who serves. For who is greater, the one who is at the table or the one who serves? Is it not the one who is at the table? But I am among you as one who serves" (Luke 22:25-27).

Certainly, we recognize that we are sinners. We will always fall short of being the persons we would like to be. The real question is whether we will own up to the fact that we are guilty as charged. Or will we continue to look around, innocently asking the question, "Surely not I?" Deep down we already know the truth. We have betrayed our Lord. But Jesus died to take away even that sin. As sinners who have been accepted because of Jesus' work, we put down the proud sinful nature every day. And when we fall, we ask God for forgiveness and for strength to live every day as those who are proud to be called his own.

WARM FAMILY MEMORIES OF EASTERS LONG AGO

When I was a kid in California, I lived on a citrus and cattle ranch. During the Easter season, poppies and lupines covered the hills north of our house—a giant orange and purple carpet dotted with sagebrush and rocks. When the early morning sun first shone on those hills, and a gentle breeze rustled through those thousands of flowers, my young mind could imagine nothing more beautiful. Occasionally, a clump of pure white hybrid lupines would stand, innocent and special, among all the other flowers. At Easter they reminded me of the sacrifice of the innocent One, made so that we might live. The flowers in our personal garden were also at their brightest and best at Easter.

Easter was always a special time for our family. It meant getting chocolate Easter bunnies and colored jelly beans. Easter meant getting new clothes so we could look our best when we went to church. We were far from wealthy—materially—but at this time of year, my parents, my siblings, and I really tried to look our very best.

The church somehow always looked its best at Easter too. With its stucco exterior, red Spanish tile roof, bell tower, and stained-glass windows, it was something to see. And the grounds were manicured just so for Easter day. Inside, at the front of the church, the early morning sun divided into a magnificent spectrum of colored light as it passed through the circular stained-glass window.

On Easter Sunday, the church would invariably be so full we had to open up the extra space behind the curtain at the back. Even then the last people in had a hard time finding a seat.

Easter meant beautiful hymns about the risen Lord, led by the choir director and sung with gusto by 250-plus voices. Those songs were contagious, upbeat, joyous, and fun. I can still hear those songs when I let my mind drift back over the years. Just as uplifting was the inspiring sermon about the risen Lord, who died and came back from the grave so we might live. Before the offering, the whole congregation would sing the doxology. It was simply awesome! I still get goose bumps on the back of my neck and sometimes choke up when we sing that verse in church.

After church, my father would begin our big family meal with a prayer. All these years since his death, I have tried to remember the exact words he used. I do remember they included words of thanksgiving and a petition to watch over our family.

Later in the day, we often went for a picnic on the hillsides above our house. There we enjoyed the sun, flowers, and solitude, while we played games and hunted for hidden eggs.

Make Easter a special celebration for your family. Put on your best clothes, bring your best singing voice, and fill your church with the sounds of those favorite old hymns. With your fellow Easter pilgrims, hear the joyful message of the risen Savior, and make the rafters ring to his glory. Celebrate the risen Lord, who offers us salvation, not just on Easter but every day of the year.

POLISHED WHITE SHOES

A number of things come to mind whenever someone mentions Easter. At the top of the list for me is one that may seem unusual to others. Shoes—new, white dress shoes. When I was young, my mother and almost all the other women at the Easter worship service would wear shiny white shoes with their Easter outfits. In my young mind, polished white shoes and the celebration of Easter went hand in hand. Because we lived in the country, shoes didn't stay clean very long. But on Easter morning as we headed out the door for church, those shoes would be shining a high glossy white.

As I think back over many Easters, the message illustrated by those carefully polished white dress shoes shines through—a message that proclaims the precious truth: Christ died on the cross to cleanse us of our sins.

The psalmist said, "Surely I was sinful at birth, sinful from the time my mother conceived me" (Psalm 51:5), and "Wash me, and I will be whiter than snow" (verse 7). Like those white shoes from Easters past, we sinners are in constant need of cleansing. Our cleansing came through the death and resurrection of Jesus. Isaiah spoke of that cleansing already 750 years before it happened. "Though your sins are like scarlet, they shall be as white as snow" (1:18). Our sins have been washed away—we have been made as white as snow. When Jesus emerged from the tomb that first Easter, it was with the assurance that our forgiveness had been won. Our cleansing had been accomplished.

In our family, to wear white shoes on Easter required a certain sacrifice. Money was short and dress shoes were expensive. But we looked at it as a wonderful way to celebrate the greatest sacrifice ever made, that Jesus gave up his life on the cross to pay for our sins. We have every reason to give thanks every day, for he has blessed us with a marvelous privilege. Christ says in Revelation 3:4,5: "They will walk with me, dressed in white, for they are worthy. He who overcomes will, like them, be dressed in white. I will never blot out his name from the book of life, but will acknowledge his name before my Father and his angels."

Whenever you see a pair of shiny white shoes, may you remember the story of polished, white Easter shoes and the joyful truth to which they point: Our sins are forgiven! Hallelujah!

FOR THOSE LEFT BEHIND

As Ruth and I entered later middle age, we found that we were attending more and more funerals for loved ones and people we knew. Every day we were faced with evidence of our own mortality. When people ask how I am doing, I often respond jokingly, "Every morning I check the obituaries in the paper. If I am not there, I figure I am good for another day!" That usually gets a smile. But down deep I know that as each day goes by, I am one day closer to home.

When we are young, the end of life seems so far away, we barely pay attention to it. With youth comes the feeling of invincibility. But age brings a reality check. Perhaps that is why we see a higher percentage of older people in church. The Lord allots to each of us a certain time of grace on this earth. He knows the number of our days. As we age, we come to realize that many of those days have already been used.

Easter is a good time to look to the end of our lives on earth, because Easter promises a better life beyond death. When we lose a loved one or a friend, we may have a hard time understanding why. But if our loved one knew that Jesus is the Savior, we know that he or she is now in a happier, better place with the Lord.

When one such loss touched our lives a few years ago, Ruth wrote this poem:

For Those Left Behind

It is hard to understand the Lord's calling
In terms of our loved one's going and our staying.
But the Lord's love is ever present
In his Word and in the friendship and love
Of friends and family.

We grieve for our loved ones because we miss them and want to be with them. Because we have the promise of Easter, we know we will see our Christian friends again one day. Because Christ died for our sins and rose again, all believers have eternal life through him.

Yes, the last day of our lives steps closer every day. That truth reminds us of our all-important task of pointing our friends and loved ones to Jesus and his saving grace all throughout their lives. And as we speak to others of the hope that is ours in Christ Jesus, we trust that the Holy Spirit will work in their hearts.

We also look for opportunities to care for members of our church family by comforting others when loved ones are lost. We have the one gift that can truly give comfort, even in the deepest sorrow. "Come to me, all you who are weary and burdened, and I will give you rest" (Matthew 11:28).

THE KIY (KEY) TO LIFE

Just what does Easter mean to you? Do you think of spring, nice weather, colored eggs, bonnets, baskets, candy, big meals, or pretty flowers just coming into bloom? Does Easter mean going to church for a special Easter service?

Easter is all of these things and so much more! Because Christ died for our sins on Good Friday and defeated the grave on Easter, we have hope that makes all the difference. We have the sure hope of an eternal home with God in heaven. You see, Jesus is the Kiy to life. No, I didn't misspell *key*. My son, Greg, did that back in 1976 when he burned this truth onto a piece of old wood with a wood-burning tool. That plaque was a special expression of his faith.

As a small boy Greg had learned the Easter story. A sensitive and thoughtful person, he asked me one evening how and why people could have treated Jesus that way. That was a tough question. I answered it as well as I could. Greg went on to study the Bible and the life of Jesus in church, Bible camp, and Sunday school. As he did, the Holy Spirit was able to nurture the seed of faith that had been planted at his baptism when he was an infant.

If you ask me what Easter means to me, I'll tell you: Jesus is the Kiy to life. It means that although Greg was taken home to be with his Lord when he was just short of 13 years of age, I will see my son again. We still miss him terribly. But every Easter when I see that old piece of wood and its inscription: "Jesus is the Kiy to life," I am reminded we will be together again soon—all because of Christ's death and resurrection.

This is not a sad story. It is a joyous one! Have a wonderful Easter! Remember, Easter is truly a beautiful day because Jesus is the Kiy to life!

Response to a Letter from Jim

Dear Jim,

Yes, I remember.

I remember the cool, crisp smell of wild oats and sage-brush at 5:00 A.M. when my father roused this six-year-old out of bed to hunt deer with him on our ranch.

I remember Monte Montana, cowboy movie star and trick roper, coming to our grade school with trick riders, trick ropers, and a full-sized stagecoach and horses. I knew right then that I would always love horses and cowboys.

I remember driving the tractor at age 6 to move farm equipment.

I remember how my dad threw pebbles on our tin roof early each Christmas morning, so we kids could hear the reindeer. I can still picture the glow of the lighted tree and the glow on our faces as my brother, my sister, and I saw the wonderful gifts around the tree. I can still hear the mellow tones of Bing Crosby floating from an old record player as he sang "Silent Night" and other Christmas favorites.

I remember that though we were poor like everyone, we dressed in our very best for church on Sunday morning because that was the respectful thing to do.

I remember when my folks took the time to take us to the beach, and I can remember the retreating waves pulling the sand through my toes.

And, yes, I remember radio shows like *Superman* and *Clyde Beatty,* starring the animal trainer (back when I still believed all circuses treated animals well). I remember *Fibber McGee and Molly, Amos 'n Andy, The Jack Benny Show* (when we were able to laugh and cry without the need for profanity), *The Green Hornet,* and *Dragnet* (when the police were still respected). I remember that justice came swiftly on *Gunsmoke.*

I remember the last gift to come from behind the Christmas tree when I was 12. How thrilled I was with that old open-sight Model 94 Winchester 30-30, which my grandfather had so lovingly oiled and polished. It was my first deer rifle.

I remember my folks saying that the president of the United States was a man to respect.

I remember when riding my horse four miles to town with friends was considered great entertainment.

I remember working on various ranches for nine to ten hours a day for 90 cents an hour—and being thankful I had that summer job.

I remember the simple beauty of the rippling lupines, poppies, and other wild flowers on the hillsides behind our home in the spring.

I remember the spirit and beauty of the Christmas and Easter services in my small home church.

I remember horseback riding for miles in sunshine or rain, daylight or darkness—for the sheer fun of it. I remember studying the stars as I rode at night, singing or whistling melodies like "Kumbaya" and "Do Lord."

I remember the Martin and Osa Johnson films that featured wonderful pictures of the animals of Africa. With a heavy heart, I remember pictures of the great migrating herds that have disappeared from that continent forever.

I remember evenings spent hiking through the hills, hearing nothing but the sound of my boots, the wind in the trees, and the soft call of mourning doves.

I remember the wonderful meals my mother cooked every Sunday after church and the words of thanksgiving my father offered to our generous God. And I remember the fun target practice sessions with Dad and Grandfather after dinner was done.

I remember the sound of the oak branches scraping against the old tin-covered building that served as my bedroom for several years. I remember the tremendous amount of work my father and grandfather did in order to drag that old building from the hilltop a mile away, to a spot near our house. My folks did that all because they wanted me to have my own room. I remember the wood stove I used for heat. It filled the room with smoke when it was first lit and then with an amazing amount of heat when it finally got going. I remember how my father built a bathroom and closet onto that old tin room. He did the work all by himself using the skills a jack-of-all-trades rancher developed out of necessity.

I remember a grandfather who had time to teach me to appreciate the wonders of nature, the value of a fine firearm, and the art of hunting.

I remember the smell of the cookies hot out of Grandma's oven. The cookies always just happened to be ready for us kids when we walked by on the mile-long journey from the bus stop.

I remember a lot of love for family and God. I remember the members of my extended family, who generally attended church each Sunday and who often helped with church projects and activities.

Yes, I remember often. And when I do, I sometimes get tears in my eyes and a lump in my throat, because I know much of it is gone forever. Yet even these nostalgic ramblings, which bring an occasional tear to my eye, are a confession of God's grace. In this hurry-up world, it is so easy to forget the everyday blessings that have filled our lives. It is easy to forget that although some of those people and blessings are gone now, God is still with us. His mercy and compassion "are new every morning" (Lamentations 3:23).

In his first letter, the apostle Peter wrote about the fleeting nature of this life. As I look back on my fleeting life, I see, even more clearly, how true and how comforting are his words: "All men are like grass, and all their glory is like the flowers of the field; the grass withers and the flowers fall, but the word of the Lord stands forever" (1 Peter 1:24,25).

Thoughts from an old man,
John H.